Inclusive Design for Products

Including your **missing 20%** by embedding
web and mobile accessibility

Prof. Jonathan Hassell

R3THINK PRESS

First published in Great Britain in 2019 by Rethink Press
(www.rethinkpress.com)

Cover design Natalie Kaaserer

Praise

'For someone who is looking to begin the process of implementing accessibility practice into their organisation, I see this volume as essential.'

> – **Jennison Asuncion**, Head of Accessibility Engineering Evangelism, LinkedIn and Founder of the Global Accessibility Awareness Day

'Jonathan Hassell is one of the shining lights of the global digital accessibility campaign. Now, with his own company, Hassell Inclusion, he has done the very thing many professionals dread doing: he has taken the time and effort to put everything he knows into a book so that anyone with influence over the way digital systems are designed can ensure disabled people are included in the digital future. This is not a dry, difficult read; the writing is human, personable and from the perspective of one who understands the challenges ahead, but believes a better future is well within our collective grasp. Congratulations, Jonathan, for bringing this important book into being. I hope it gets the wide readership it deserves.'

— **Julie Howell**, Lead Author of PAS 78

'This is an outstanding resource. I can't wait to start embedding the advice in this book into my daily work flow. I've done a lot of work within accessibility, but this definitely helps bring me to another level.'

— **Chris Loiselle**, Accessibility Team Lead, Perkins School for the Blind and Invited Expert W3C

'A book that should be on the shelf of every head designer or strategist of any company that sells a product or government agency that seeks to include all of its employees and constituents. Jonathan Hassell spent hundreds of hours interviewing the leaders in this field. They are, like Hassell, passionate about their involvement in taking on the limitations imposed by the digital environment for people who need alternative access. Their enthusiasm quickly becomes your own. Their solutions are shared freely, for your benefit – you can use them for your own business or agency. Whatever your corporate task is related to accessibility, there will be a chapter and practical information on how to implement small and big changes that make a difference.'

> – **Elianna James**, Director of Accessibility Training, Be Accessible Inc.

'I've found this book such a practical guide to getting accessibility actually embedded in a large commercial organisation. Reading it while in the midst of leading an accessibility transformation programme really helped me clarify my thinking on what our goals were, and why we needed to prioritise some outcomes over others. It gave me ideas to help persuade people at all levels of the organisation, as well as a step-by-step guide to adjusting our existing roles and processes to include accessibility considerations. Using it helped me create a practical, sustainable process for accessibility that was focused on our customers' priorities.'

> – **Maura Moran**, Senior Content Consultant

Contents

Foreword   xi

Preface To The Second Edition   xv

Introduction   1
   Note on language   7
   Support materials to accompany this book   9

PART ONE THE APPROACH   11

1 The Hassell Inclusion Way Of Implementing
  ISO 30071-1   13
   Expand awareness   15
   Embed strategy   20
   Enable process   23
   Measure effects   28
   Continually evolve   36
   ISO 30071-1: your shortcut to accessibility
       maturity   42
   What digital products, hybrid products and
       ICT systems does ISO 30071-1 cover?   45
   How this book expands on ISO 30071-1   47

2 Enable Process – How To Embed Accessibility in Your Digital Product Development Lifecycle Process   **51**

Why the current approach isn't working   52

How ISO 30071-1 helps   54

How ISO 30071-1's activities can improve your
  process   55

How to integrate ISO 30071-1's activities into
  your process   62

How ISO 30071-1 helps you make justifiable
  decisions   65

How to document your decisions   70

PART TWO THE ACTIVITIES   **79**

1 Specify The Widest Range Of Potential Users   81

a. Define your product's target audiences   82

b. Understanding disabled user groups   91

c. Define the relationship the product will
  have with its audiences   109

2 Specify User Goals And Tasks   115

a. Specify the purpose of the product   116

b. Split the product's user goals and tasks into
  core and non-core   121

c. Understanding how disabled people use
  digital products   126

d. Noting the technology preferences and
  restrictions of the product's target
  audiences   136

e. The impact of the device(s) that your
   product will support   145

3 Specify User Accessibility Needs   **163**
a. Integrating people with disabilities into
   your user research   164
b. Defining success criteria and setting the
   level of accessibility experience   173
c. Defining your target browsers and assistive
   technologies   185

4 Specify Accessibility Requirements   **197**
a. Specify your product's implementation
   technologies   199
b. Specify your product's enabling
   technologies   202
c. Using technical accessibility guidelines to
   specify accessibility requirements   209
d. Using your accessibility requirements to
   procure the product or outsource its
   creation   236

5 Specify Design Approach   **257**
a. Your options when a single-design approach
   doesn't work   262
b. Situations where accessibility via the
   accessibility ecosystem isn't available   269

6 Ensure Accessibility Requirements Are Met   **277**
a. Assure the product's accessibility through
   implementation planning   278

b. Assure the product's accessibility through
    testing   288
c. Making decisions about launch from an
    accessibility point of view   320

7 Ensure Communication About Accessibility   **329**
a. Creating your accessibility statement   330
b. What can happen if you get your
    communication wrong   335

8 Ensure Integration Of Accessibility In System
Updates   **339**
a. Proactive activity: upholding accessibility
    during minor product maintenance   340
b. Proactive activity: upholding accessibility
    when making new releases of the product   347
c. Reactive activity: responding to changes in
    technology after launch   352
d. Reactive activity: responding to accessibility
    feedback   354

What's Next?   **359**

References   **361**

Acknowledgements   **369**

The Author   **373**

Foreword

L ong ago, when dinosaurs ruled the earth, in 2007, Jonathan Hassell and I sat in a room with a group of accessibility experts at the British Standards Institution HQ in Gunnersbury, West London, to begin work on drafting what became 'BS 8878:2010 Web accessibility. Code of practice', and which would be extended in May 2019 to become an international standard, snappily titled 'ISO/IEC 30071-1: Code of practice for creating accessible ICT products and services'.

Much has changed over the last twelve years. Dinosaurs died out (mostly). My hair turned grey, while Jonathan seemingly didn't age at all. But most importantly, it became easier to explain to people the business benefits of making accessible products and services. Instead of seeing accessibility as merely a matter of complying with disability discrimination legislation to avoid being sued, businesses started to understand that accessibility is not about making special efforts to accommodate disabled people, but about ensuring that products and services are inclusive – making them as available to as many potential customers as possible.

For example, in their 2016 paper 'Implementing Recommendations From Web Accessibility Guidelines: Would They Also Provide Benefits to Nondisabled Users', Sven Schmutz, Andreas Sonderegger and Juergen Sauer concluded that accessible websites are better for non-disabled users:

> 'Sixty-one non-disabled participants used one of three Web sites differing in levels of accessibility (high, low, and very low) … A high level of Web accessibility led to better performance (i.e. task completion time and task completion rate) than low or very low accessibility. Likewise, high Web accessibility improved user ratings (i.e. perceived usability, aesthetics, workload, and trustworthiness) compared to low or very low Web accessibility.'[1]

At the same time, companies in Level 4 economies (what we used to call 'the West' or 'developed economies') are becoming aware of the commercial importance of the world outside their own borders. By 2027, a seismic shift in the world will have occurred: the number of rich consumers outside the West will have risen from 40% (in 2017) to 50%. By 2040, 60% of the world's richest consumers will be from non-Western nations.[2] This is due to two factors: the rising disposable income of Level 3 nations, and the growing populations of Asia and Africa. The United Nations predicts that by 2050 the population of Asia will double from 1 billion to 2 billion, and the population of Africa will similarly rise from 1 to 2 billion people. Meanwhile, the population of the West will remain static.[3]

When I started working for Opera (a browser that largely served people in India, Indonesia, Nigeria, Russia and similar Level 2 and 3 economies) in 2008, it was very difficult for me to persuade companies to adjust their websites to work in the Opera Mini browser. But gradually that changed; by the end of my time at the company in 2016, organisations would be actively seeking me out to ask how they could make sure their sites worked in our browsers.

The answer I gave them was simple: ensure that sites are small, their images are compressed, the HTML code they use is robust and they are built accessibly. Largely, the technical rules for including people with disabilities work just as well for including people on older or lower-powered devices over slow networks.

The technical guidelines for making inclusive accessible sites are not especially complex. But they need to be implemented in an environment that supports the developers. Business processes need to be put in place to ensure that accessibility is built into ICT projects from the start: developers need training; content authors need to provide information in accessible formats; project managers need to factor in iterative accessibility testing, and so forth.

This book shows you how to use the fruits of our labour – ISO 30071-1 – to cement accessibility into your organisation: how to embed the right mindsets, processes and procedures into your wider business to support the development of products and services that can reach more and more people in our ever-shifting, internationalised global marketplace.

There's never been a better time to make that happen.

Bruce Lawson
Web standards, HTML, CSS and accessibility expert, trainer and consultant
Former Deputy Chief Technology Officer, Opera

Preface To The Second Edition

Inclusive design is now cool. It's 'so hot right now'.

In LinkedIn's '50 Big Ideas for 2019', inclusive design was number 6, just below Brexit, just above artificial intelligence (AI). And don't just take their word for it. Take Satya Nadella's, or Tim Cook's, or any of the other senior execs talking about it at the likes of Google, IBM or Facebook.

According to Satya Nadella, '2019 is the year inclusive design goes mainstream'.

Why?

Inclusive design is a new way of talking about accessibility, which accessibility advocates have been talking about for decades. So, what has suddenly made it so exciting, rather than something many people do because they feel they have to? If tech giants like Apple and Microsoft are investing in it heavily, should you too? What are the benefits for you in your organisation – whether you're a retailer that uses the web for selling what you make, a marketing agency creating mobile apps for clients, or a tiny not-for-profit promoting yourself on social media?

Accessibility advocates are thrilled that inclusive design is now getting all this attention. But some people are rightly asking if it's here for the long term, or if it's just a fad. If you invest lots of money in it now, will it be the best decision you made this year, or something you'll regret in a few years?

These are the right questions to be asking right now. I'd suggest the people answering them should be those who've been working towards becoming mature in digital accessibility for almost twenty years now. People who've been through the learning curve, made the mistakes and learnt from them, so you don't have to. People like those who gathered together at ISO and BSI to put their experience into ISO 30071-1, and BS 8878 before that. People who

read the first edition of this book in 2014 and have
been getting good at this ever since.

I believe this book, and its companion *Inclusive
Design for Organisations*, which together explain
ISO 30071-1, are a great way to understand the value
of inclusive design for your organisation and embed
it into your thinking, culture, policies and product
processes. I hope it helps your organisation become
inclusive in a way that doesn't cost you the earth,
so you can start enjoying the benefits of inclusive
design for your market segment and product type.

– **Jonathan Hassell**

Introduction

M ost organisations are oblivious to, or terrified
about, digital accessibility.

They're probably aware that up to 20% of their
customers – people with disabilities – could be
clicking away from their websites or leaving their
mobile apps every day, without having bought
anything or found the information or service they
wished to find, never to return. They may even have
heard from some of this 20%, complaining about
problems they can't understand, asking for what
seem like impossible fixes when their teams are
already overloaded with much-needed new feature
development. They know there's the possibility
they'll be sued if they don't do the right thing, but
they don't know how far they need to go to prevent
that.

While some tech giants are investing in inclusive design, they don't know if there's anything in it for them other than risk mitigation against laws that seem to be constantly changing, that don't line up internationally, and for which they can find precious little case law to constitute a credible legal threat (unless they are in the United States). They're anxious to know what their competitors are doing, whether this is an area in which they should be a leader or follower, and what the value of accessibility would be (possibly as a unique selling point (USP)) if they invested in it. Their web teams may have read the industry standard Web Content Accessibility Guidelines (WCAG) but found them impenetrable and badly organised. Worse, when their designers do locate the 'success criteria' for design, the guidelines seem like a creative straitjacket that tells them everything they can't do, but little about why.

Accessibility, it seems, is a cul-de-sac that organisations are being legally blackmailed into spending time on, which will result in products that are better for the 20% of people with disabilities and worse for the 80% who are not disabled. Moreover, they have no idea how many disabled people are actually using their site or app, or how many more will because they're now spending good money making it more accessible. So if they do make something 'accessible', it's usually only for one product or one version of a product. And it's usually because of one committed, passionate 'accessibility superhero' on the team whose departure would leave them needing to start all over again.

If this sounds like where you work, I have some comforting news: you are not alone.

I learnt where I believe most organisations want to be directly from the heads of diversity and inclusion of the top blue-chip corporations in Europe at a meeting of the Vanguard Network early in 2011. I was speaking for the BBC at the event on the innovation possibilities of web accessibility for inclusion, but before I could start, the event's chair did something amazing. She spent a whole hour going around the room, asking each of the delegates what one thing would really make a difference to their organisation's inclusion practices if they could achieve it. When they were asked to vote for which of the contributions each felt was the most important, this was the unanimous choice:

> 'What I want is to strategically embed inclusion into my organisation's culture and business-as-usual processes, rather than just doing *another* inclusion project.'

If you were sitting opposite me at the event, you'd
have seen my mouth open wide in recognition: the
British standard that I and so many other people had
laboured on for three years was exactly what those
in the room were asking for, at least when it came to
their organisation's digital presence.

I spent much of my lunchtime conveying to the
people in the room that:

- They could implement a strategy that would
  allow them to attract and keep the 20% of their
  audience who are disabled, while not detracting
  from the user experience of those who aren't

- There was a way they could sleep soundly,
  knowing that they'd done enough to cover their
  'accessibility risk' without it costing the earth

- Through following a simple, strategic business-
  aligned framework, they could embed the best
  practice necessary to *consistently* achieve these
  aims throughout their organisation and digital
  products

- The framework would allow them to align
  accessibility and usability within their product
  teams, showing them when both could be
  achieved together and when the user needs of

different groups would require them to add personalisation to their products

- All of this work could benefit their organisation, not just in risk mitigation, customer service and corporate social responsibility, but also in their bottom line as benchmarked analytics show how disabled and older people's use of their sites could increase their turnover and profits

What did I have that could take these people's organisations from their position of pain to the place they all wanted to be? The standard that I'd just led the creation of for the British Standards Institution (BSI). British Standard (BS) 8878:2010 *Web Accessibility – Code of Practice*. BS 8878 opened up in detail the strategies, policies and processes that award-winning, best-of-breed organisations like the BBC, IBM, Vodafone, Opera, BT and Lloyds Banking Group have used to become 'accessibility competent and confident' so that they can be used by any organisation, no matter how big or small.

One month later, I was at a conference of international accessibility standards experts at BSI in London, chatting with people from Japan and Canada who told me that they had an immediate need for the standard in their countries. These conversations took me on an eight-year journey to deliver what they were asking for – *ISO 30071-1,* which is the internationalisation and extension of BS 8878. It was launched in May 2019, prompting the second edition of this book.

ISO 30071-1 has arrived at a time when some of the largest companies on the planet – including Apple, Google and Microsoft – are recognising that inclusive design is an idea that needs to go mainstream. Tablet and smartphone vendors are racing to promote accessibility as a key selling point of their devices. The legal imperatives behind accessibility are being strengthened internationally and the number of cases being brought against inaccessible websites is rising at a huge rate.

We are also entering a massive demographic change as baby boomers all over the world start to need some of the same accessibility features that disabled people have always needed. As our populations age, the number of people who need accessibility is rocketing up – the 'missing 20%' is rapidly becoming 'the missing 40%'.

There's never been a better time to get good at digital accessibility, especially as people who have embedded BS 8878 within their production processes are increasingly telling me that its user-centred inclusive design thinking has resulted in not only *more accessible* websites and apps for disabled people, but *better* websites and apps for everyone. On top of that, I have numerous stories of how the inclusive design thinking in BS 8878 and ISO 30071-1 has helped organisations be more innovative in their product ideation, which is why I was in the room with the Vanguard Network in the first place.

So I'm hoping you, like the Vanguard Network, will want to know more...

Note on language

You'll find I interchange between the words 'accessibility' and 'inclusion' throughout this book. I will sometimes use 'accessibility' as it's the word most people know, but I prefer 'inclusion' as it avoids one of the main pitfalls that people who care about ensuring those with disabilities are not excluded can fall into: they care so much about how easy it is for people with disabilities to use products, they forget about the needs of people without disabilities using the same product. For them, accessibility is the *most* important aspect of the product, not *an* important aspect of the product.

I believe sacrificing the needs of the majority non-disabled audience to uphold the needs of the minority of people with disabilities is always the wrong thing to do. It's unsustainable. It doesn't allow *everyone* to win. It just swaps the people who win from being people without disabilities to being people with disabilities.

That's not a good enough goal. The goal should always be to make products work for everyone, rather than saying that's the goal, and then acting like disabled audiences are more important than any other audience, spurred on by guidelines that don't take the impact of every checkpoint on non-disabled users and project budgets adequately into account.

Inclusive design or 'universal design' is at the heart of ISO 30071-1. It reminds everyone to consider *all* user groups. And it benefits all user groups, because when it asks digital product owners to think about people with disabilities who are so different from themselves, they become sensitive to the needs of people who are only a little different to themselves – ageing parents, for example. Going the extra mile makes them more sensitive to everyone's needs, which can only be a good thing.

Support materials to accompany this book

This book contains many important lessons that some of the world's most successful accessibility experts learnt when they embedded a framework for accessibility competence in their organisation. To help you put their advice into practice in your organisation, I've created a wealth of free resources to help you complete the practical exercises I've included at the end of most sections of the book:

- Tools and templates that you can use to quickly get started with:

  - Generating a tailored accessibility business case for your organisation

  - Creating your organisational information and communications technology (ICT) accessibility policy

  - Creating ICT system accessibility logs for your digital products

  - Prioritising issues that get uncovered by accessibility testing

- Access to Hassell Inclusion's latest podcasts and blogs, which are refreshed weekly

- Information on training, webinars and support forums

This book is just the start. Get help for the rest of your journey from http://qrs.ly/3a4a6bm or use the QR code below:

PART ONE

THE APPROACH

CHAPTER 1

The Hassell Inclusion Way Of Implementing ISO 30071-1

et's start with an overview of the different stages of the journey towards digital accessibility competence and confidence that most organisations could benefit from. At Hassell Inclusion, we like to call these the Five Keys to unlock solutions to critical elements of digital accessibility maturity:

1. *Expand awareness* – expanding your thinking about how your organisation can benefit from inclusive design

2. *Embed strategy* – embedding inclusion as a value and competence across all parts of your

organisation, so all your staff and policies are working together to gain you those benefits

3. *Enable process* – enabling your digital production teams to create products that are inclusive by embedding accessibility in their process

4. *Measure effects* – measuring the effect all of this has on your organisation's users/customers, brand reputation and bottom line

5. *Continually evolve* – planning how to evolve your accessibility thinking and practice as technology changes, and how you can evolve technology yourself through innovations that come from engaging with different people's access needs

You can find detail on each of these stages in this book's companion: *Inclusive Design for Organisations*. Here I'll summarise each by way of a real-world story.

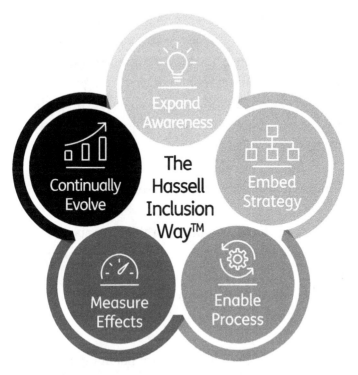

The Five Keys to The Hassell Inclusion Way

Expand awareness

It's critical to use the first key before you go any further in your journey towards accessibility competence and confidence. If you don't expand your thinking, your whole organisation will be unsure of the reasoning behind the training, governance, policies or processes you introduce.

You'll be taking your staff on a journey that will involve them learning new skills, working in new ways and changing 'the way things are done around here' without telling them why any change is necessary, what the point of the change is and when it will be over. Even worse, your organisation may start on a journey because 'that's what everyone else is doing' and end up in the wrong destination because it is actually different from 'everyone else'.

The first key is expanding your thinking about why you should go on the journey at all – examining the reasons and motivations for doing it to find which best fit your organisation's culture, purposes and products or services.

There are lots of good reasons for behaving in a certain way, but if you're unsure of your motivation, you will be forever second-guessing how you should behave when the journey gets difficult.

Let me tell you a story.

Have you ever been in a traffic jam?

Imagine me in my 2002-model blue Ford Focus – the most inclusively designed car of all time – at 11.15 on a crisp morning in January. I'm just coming out of a traffic jam that has been frustrating me for the last thirty minutes. But finally, the road ahead looks clear.

I should be feeling relieved.

Today is my mother's birthday – that's the reason why my family and I are on this motorway. And it's the reason why I'm still frustrated, because between me and the clear road ahead is a figure that is stressing me out. The figure is one of the main reasons why I bought my satnav. It's the one thing that no satnav will ever be sold without.

It's the estimated time of arrival (ETA).

My mother's birthday lunch is booked for 12.15. The ETA says 12.30. So, what does my right foot do?

Five minutes later, another aspect of my satnav comes into play – the speed-camera detection, which shows me a camera is coming up. Why is this a problem? Because I'm not going at the speed limit, like pretty much every other car I can see on the road. So I slow down. But for how long? Ten minutes? One minute? No, more like fifteen seconds. Because as soon as I'm past the camera, my right foot takes over again.

Why this behaviour? Why am I not going at the speed limit when everything says that I should? The law says that I should be going slower. I know it's the 'right thing to do' – it would be better for the environment, and safer for my wife and son sitting in the back of the car. It would even be cheaper for me, over time helping me save money which I could spend on whatever I wanted...

But no, all of these motivations are outweighed by my ETA. That's what's driving me. Anything else is a distraction I'll work around.

Compare this situation with the roads in Norway. If my colleagues at an accessibility conference in Oslo are correct, there the authorities seem to actually understand human behaviour. In Norway, speed cameras take photos of all the cars that go past them, not just those that are speeding, because you don't pay your speeding fines to a faceless bureaucrat in a government office somewhere; you pay them to the people who were going under the speed limit past the same speed camera on the same day.

In Norway, a speed camera can be your friend. It can even make you money. You can win.

So, where would you prefer to drive? England? Or Norway?

That's just a simple example to show why it's necessary to reframe the accessibility conversation. For too long, digital accessibility has been considered to be all about avoiding losing. All about getting away with as little as possible, doing only what you absolutely have to do to avoid getting into legal trouble. Riding your luck. The best thing that could happen is that you successfully get away with ignoring it, because there's nothing to win. Buying the cheapest accessibility insurance policy you can, because you're not convinced that you'll ever need it.

That's not motivational to anyone other than your risk management department.

To be worth doing at all, accessibility needs to be considered in the right way. With 20% to 40% of your potential audience caring about how you handle the accessibility of your products, it isn't about avoiding losing, it's about winning. Winning a bigger audience. Winning better brand reputation. Just plain old winning.

Now that sounds far more interesting, doesn't it?

You can find more details on this key in Chapter 3 of *Inclusive Design for Organisations*. This details how to expand the way you think about accessibility, so that you can understand its relative importance to your organisation when compared with all the other aspects of product design and, as a result, provide a much more stable, reliable motivation for spending time on it.

Embed strategy

Once you've expanded your thinking to encompass better motivation for accessibility, the second key is critical to ensure that you can actually *deliver it* in the culture and structure of your organisation. This is about identifying all the things that need to work together to make sure you deliver the accessibility you want efficiently, and that nothing snatches defeat from the jaws of success.

I'm talking about embedding inclusion as a value that pervades your organisation. Like a stick of seaside rock, a cross section of any aspect of your organisation should show the same values at play. Not only is there nothing that could derail your ability to deliver to your values, but there is understanding, competence and confidence present that this is worth doing and achievable.

To give you an analogy from a sport I took up after I was spurred on by Britain's successes in the 2012

London Olympics, let's consider how rowing teams win.

Firstly, everyone in the boat has the same goal – to go in the same direction as quickly as possible. There's not much chance for an individual rower to do otherwise with only one oar in their hands, but they could turn the oar over and try to push the water the other way if they wanted to slow the whole team down. And yes, a couple of times on my early outings in the boat, a number of us novices inadvertently ended up doing just that. Not because we wanted to, but because we were concentrating on another part of our stroke at the time.

Secondly, everyone in the boat is doing their job, not someone else's. There are effectively three jobs in the boat: the one 'stroke' rower is establishing the rowers' rhythm; the other seven rowers are rowing to that rhythm; and the one cox is steering and providing feedback to each rower on how they need to tweak their performance to stick to that rhythm. If two people try to steer the boat, say by stopping rowing on one side so the boat turns against its rudder, it's fighting against itself. If a rower who isn't 'stroke' decides to set a different rhythm, say by rowing faster to make the boat go faster, this actually slows the boat down and confuses the whole crew. If an inexperienced or lower-skilled rower doesn't pay attention to feedback from the cox on how they are rowing, an unchecked increase in the depth their blade goes into the water could unbalance the boat and end up rocking it up and down, resulting in the other rowers needing to work to stabilise it rather than concentrating on powering forwards.

Thirdly, the equipment the team is using could sabotage the enterprise. A great crew, harmonised in purpose, rhythm and technique, can be beaten by a group of novices if there's a leak in the boat.

And finally, a winning team can slowly go off the boil if they feel that the club they row for is taking them for granted. They may feel that new club leaders are more interested in other parts of running the club, assuming that the team will always win even if they aren't given the time to practise or feedback on any bad habits that might be creeping into their game.

The same is true for any organisation – for it to succeed in its goal, all of its members need to agree on the goal; understand their role in working towards it; be trained in how to perform that role; and have someone providing feedback on how they are performing, both to correct errors or inefficiencies, and to allow them to recognise and feel appreciated for great performance.

Traditional accessibility guidelines have concentrated almost exclusively on what developers, designers and content creators (the seven ordinary rowers in our analogy) need to do to deliver accessibility, without understanding that their work can be either facilitated or hindered by the layers of more strategic management and policy above them.

You can find more details on this key in Chapter 4 of *Inclusive Design for Organisations*, which looks at ways of embedding accessibility as a value, goal and competence in all the people and policies in your organisation who have an impact on whether your products are made to be accessible.

Enable process

Once you've embedded accessibility as a value within your organisation's staff and policies, the third key is critical to ensure that you are able to deliver it *consistently* for all your products, whether they are similar or vary in purpose, audience, technology or importance. This is about identifying a way of working that is stable enough to ensure good accessibility results every time, while being flexible enough to handle any type of project you throw at it without breaking.

I'm talking about enabling your teams to get accessibility right, and to get it right all of the time. And to be clear, I'm not talking about a *checklist* – something that seems to be synonymous with accessibility in many people's minds; I'm talking about a *process*. A documented, flexible, repeatable process that each member of your project team buys into for every digital project your organisation runs.

As establishing a new process or change to your current process into the way you work is much more difficult to achieve than adding a checklist into your quality assurance (QA) testing, it's important for me to convince you why this is necessary. On 27 January 2012, the Royal National Institute of Blind People (RNIB) – the UK's leading vision impairment charity – served legal papers on the airline bmibaby for its failure to ensure that blind and partially sighted customers could book flights via its website.[1]

I'd like you to put yourself in bmibaby's shoes for a moment and consider what you would do in this circumstance...

I'm guessing that on the day the legal writ arrived, your web team would already be up to their necks in creating new website features or new ways of beating the competition via sales funnel conversion optimisation; getting the site to work better for people using it on a mobile phone; trying to maximise search engine optimisation (SEO) and Google pay-per-click conversions; making sure that they were monitoring Twitter and Facebook for any mentions of your organisation in the social media sphere, especially detrimental ones; pushing out the online part of marketing campaigns to sell more flights via promotions or link-ups with affiliates' websites. Each one of these to-do list items is designed to maintain or improve your organisation's visibility on the web or improve the conversion of site visitors to customers. And each one of these to-do list items needs the investment of the web team's time and energy to bring in greater revenues and profits for the company.

Into this already busy environment, the notice of legal proceedings would drop like a bombshell. And the only sensible questions to ask in response are: 'What is the minimum we need to do to make the pain go away?' and 'When do we need to do it by?' It's all hands to the pump on 'remediation' – bailing out the water in your boat and plugging the leak so you can get back to the important thing, which is sailing into the new waters already scheduled on your map.

This makes perfect sense, but it is likely to create a problem as well as solve one.

To illustrate, let me tell you the story of Achilles.

As anyone who's seen Brad Pitt's impressive combat prowess in the film *Troy* will be all too aware, Achilles was an incredible Greek warrior whose name struck fear into his opponents. He would doubtless be dismayed to find that he is renowned in modern popular culture for one part of his anatomy only: his heel.[2]

Rather than actually dealing with his one weakness, Achilles did the first century AD equivalent of putting a Band-Aid on it. This dealt with the problem immediately, but it didn't deal with it long term. And so Achilles has gone down in history as a cautionary tale, rather than being celebrated as a mighty warrior.

Why am I bringing ancient Greeks into a book on accessibility? Because fixing the accessibility problems of our website or mobile app when they are pointed out to us by an audit or user complaint is our Achilles' heel. We may want to feel that we've learnt from Achilles' unintended message to us throughout the centuries, but most organisations are treating accessibility just like a Band-Aid. Why else would 'accessibility remediation' still be such a core service from any accessibility agency?

This highlights a direct link with many organisations' limited view of the first key: expand awareness. If we're trying to 'get away with it', we'll only think of accessibility when we get caught, and then we'll rush to find the quickest, cheapest Band-Aid to make the pain go away so we can forget about it again.

The quick, cheap way of dealing with pain is the patch-up pill, not the lifestyle change that prevents the pain coming back. Yet any sensible person knows that prevention is better than cure. The fact is that we need to fix the problem in the *process* not the *product* to prevent it reoccurring.

No website or app is ever finished. Most go through content and maintenance updates every day, minor version updates weekly or monthly, and full rebuilds every couple of years. So fixing your accessibility problem in the product rather than in the way you work means that every time you upgrade your product, you may cause new accessibility problems to occur, especially as experienced product team members move on to new challenges and new team members take their place.

ISO 30071-1's best-practice advice is to enable your staff to get accessibility right all the time by embedding it in your standard digital production process, because then you will uphold accessibility not only in every new product that you create, but also in every version of those products. While embedding accessibility in your process is more challenging to accomplish than just asking one person to test the product against a checklist and do whatever fixes are necessary, its benefits are much greater.

Part Two of this book will provide a detailed journey through all the activities to put in your digital production process to consistently enable your teams to prevent accessibility problems coming up in the first place. Then pain relief isn't such a necessary part of the picture.

Measure effects

The fourth key is the one most organisations don't think about nearly enough. Often it's only something they appreciate when they think they've done everything they were supposed to do, and yet they are still faced with an email from a person with a disability accusing them of not doing the right thing. Ignoring this key can take an organisation that's done the work to get good at accessibility and turn it into one that slowly decides not to bother any more.

It is measuring the effects your accessibility work achieves. After all, if accessibility is about winning, then it is fundamentally about the effect your work has on the user experience of the disabled people you're trying to help, and the rest of your non-disabled users.

Unfortunately, this often gets forgotten, especially as checking compliance with guidelines is the one thing most people know about accessibility. This is like working out where you've come to at the end of a drive by double-checking all of the turns you made on the way, rather than by looking out of the window and asking a local where you are. You could have taken all the 'right' turns according to the map, but what if the map is a little out of date?

ISO 30071-1 uses technical accessibility standards like WCAG to do what they are good at – providing detailed instructions for how to make decisions on various technical, design and content aspects of accessibility as you create and maintain a product. What it doesn't use WCAG for is what it's not good at – telling you whether or not following those guidelines has resulted in a product that disabled people can actually use to complete the tasks they came to the site to accomplish. For this is often as much about usability and learnability as accessibility.

To highlight the importance of this, let me tell you another story, of how two days in 2008 pushed me to learn which accessibility outcomes are important for users and organisations, and which are not. Let me take you to a radio studio in BBC Broadcasting House during the hot, sticky days of summer.

If you had been sitting next to me at 2.42 one afternoon, you'd have been sitting at a green baize table looking across at the presenter of the BBC's *In Touch* radio show for people who are blind or vision impaired. He's fascinating. So much so that I'm not paying adequate attention to the frustrated voice coming through my headphones. Which is OK until it stops, the red light goes on in front of me and I realise it's my turn to speak.

This is what I'm here for: to defend the accessibility of BBC iPlayer. This shouldn't be a problem. I know we've already done the right thing. And I've prepared notes for my response. Unfortunately, unlike the Braille notes that the programme's presenter has been stroking silently under his arm as a prompt for his flawless introduction, my notes are crisply folded on the green baize in front of me, and unfolding them would be likely to create noise that would be picked up by the microphone.

So I speak from the heart.

'We really do care for blind users. We care for all our users. That's why we've found the best guidelines for how to make things work for everyone, and have followed them to the letter. We've tested the product with people with all sorts of disabilities. I even checked it with the JAWS screen reader myself this morning and…'

'So why can I not use it? Why did you have to replace something that worked with something that doesn't?'

It's a bit difficult to argue with a disembodied voice, especially live on radio. Wondering who the complaining voice belongs to, to make them more human, to have a chance of properly empathising with their position, I picture a woman in her late forties, sitting at a computer desk somewhere in middle England with a guide dog by her side. But already I'm figuring that this is a stereotype. I don't know much about her, other than she's obviously not happy. And much of what I've pictured may be completely wrong.

And then suddenly I get a flash of insight, a glimpse into her world. That's what she is actually complaining about – our product team haven't given her a good enough picture of the iPlayer we've created. The way we've designed it hasn't enabled her to understand how to use this thing she cannot see.

I'm really loving this train of thought, this insight into the needs of this user, seeing all sorts of implications for how we could…

The presenter coughs, and suddenly I'm back in the room. These insights are helpful. But they're not answering her question.

'I, er… er…'

He rescues me. 'Thankfully, not all blind users are having the same problem. Here are a number of blind people we spoke to yesterday who say that they love the product…'

The red light turns off as altogether more friendly voices soothe my ears.

The presenter gestures for me to take my headphones off. His words are for me, not our audience.

'Just a word of advice. It's not the work you do, it's whether or not it helps people that matters. Wouldn't you say?'

He's right. I've dodged a bullet as the usability and accessibility of the site – the requirements of my job – seem OK. But even going beyond guidelines and accessibility conformance and doing user testing to check the usability of our site for disabled people hasn't been enough. For this person, the *learnability* of our product is the problem. She had something that worked. We have replaced it with a version two that works in a different way, and we haven't helped her move from one to the other. And it sounds like the blind people we recruited for our testing may have been way more confident and competent in their use of the web than the majority of blind people out there. We may have been ahead of organisations that just do 'compliance'. But in reality, there's still a long way to go in our journey...

As I sit at my desk the next day, my boss places a letter in front of me as he breezes past.

'Sort this out.'

Two sentences of the first paragraph of typed text are underlined in red:

'I was disgusted to hear that you only test your sites using the JAWS screen reader. How exactly do you expect a pensioner to afford £800?'

The name on the bottom of the letter is a man's, so it's certainly not the woman from yesterday. But I have learnt from listening to her. This time I have the opportunity to engage more deeply with this user's real-world difficulties. There is more to be learnt. And this time, in private, I pick up the phone and dial the number at the bottom of the page...

Two weeks later, my team and I launch the UK's first survey into which screen readers blind people are actually using. We've bypassed asking the screen reader manufacturers and their distributors; we're talking directly to a wide variety of blind users, partnering with the RNIB to ask people on their mailing list what sort of user experience they are getting from our websites on the screen readers they use.

The time for assumptions is over: now we are going to arm ourselves with better research on which to make our decisions. And we're going to test with people who actually make up the majority of our disabled audiences, not techies whose vision impairment isn't as key to their user experience as their amazing capability to work around problems.

WCAG? It would only be the end of our journey if we didn't care whether real people were able to use the products resulting from our hard work. As we do, it's just the start.

In summary, I believe the aim of accessibility – or inclusion, as I prefer to call it – is to build a *better* product, not just a *compliant* one. Because through this lies sufficient return on investment (ROI) to make the costs of accessibility worthwhile.

That's the other effect you want to have – a positive impact on your organisation's bottom line – for accessibility to help you achieve your business goals. And a positive ROI is definitely possible.

To give one example of the bottom-line benefits of considering the needs of disabled and older people, take OXO Good Grips – a well-known American pioneer of inclusive design. Sam Farber's wife, a keen cook, suffered from arthritis, which caused her to ask him one challenging but inspiring question: 'Why do ordinary kitchen tools hurt your hands?' The result of him engaging fully with that question and how to answer it made him found OXO and created the company's fortune.[3]

The company's first fifteen products launched in 1990. They achieved sales growth of over 35% per year from 1991 to 2002. OXO's line of kitchen products has now grown to over 500 and the company has won over 100 design awards.

Now that sounds like winning to me!

You can find more details on this key in Chapter 6 of *Inclusive Design for Organisations*. 'Start with the end in mind' is always a useful policy, so measuring effects helps you ensure your accessibility strategy keeps the end firmly in mind and shows you how to measure the impact of your strategy over time, to make sure your work is having the effects you want to make it sustainable.

Continually evolve

The fifth key is one that you may think is just for organisations that are already getting good at accessibility and inclusive design. But it includes the one thing that accessibility has to potentially make your organisation rich: innovation. And you don't need to be a tech giant to do it.

It is continually evolving the way you deliver accessibility. If the fourth key allows you to prove that accessibility is worth continually investing in as you can prove it has good ROI, this is about making sure that your investment is reviewed for efficiencies and your return reviewed for opportunities.

Accessibility and inclusion are never 'done'. Technology is constantly changing and improving, so knowing how to evolve your accessibility thinking and practice is essential. What's more, thinking differently can actually help you move technology forwards. Innovation comes with the territory. If you're thinking 'We're good at this already, what's next?' then this is for you.

For inclusion to thrive in an organisation, you need to continually be reviewing the strengths, weakness, opportunities and threats in your current practices to improve the way you do it. What worked last year may not work with the latest updates in devices, operating systems (OSes), technology frameworks or design thinking. And more importantly, real opportunities to differentiate your organisation from your competitors could be hidden in the user research you've done or the accessibility challenges your teams have been facing.

What's more, if you seize those opportunities, you reframe accessibility for teams. From seeing it as a frustrating exercise in following rules that slow down product development, they will view it instead as an exercise in questioning all the established conventions of digital to create something innovative. Accessibility done well can be the sort of thing that helps you retain the best people in your organisation as you use its challenges to spark their creativity, not hinder it.

To highlight the opportunities, let me tell you another story, of how saying yes to an accessibility challenge turned into a constant stream of innovation reaching far beyond the original people it aimed to help.

In 2011, the UK advisory service on technology and inclusion JISC TechDis approached me to judge a contest to investigate how gesture recognition could help learners with disabilities who lack independence due to an inability to communicate by speech or lack of motor control. As I'd done a number of innovation projects with Gamelab UK and Reflex Arc when I was at the BBC, I decided that I didn't want to judge the contest, I wanted to win it for my new company, Hassell Inclusion.

Together, the three companies came up with a proposal for the contest and secured two phases of funding to create a Makaton sign-language recognition system to help autistic and learning-disabled Makaton users make an easier transition into independent living and employment. Hassell Inclusion led the project's user research and product design, working with specialist colleges across the UK, investigating the user contexts in which sign and gesture recognition would be both useful and appropriate for students and older adults who use Makaton. Our user research also identified ways of motivating our target users to use our evolving recognition technologies, resulting in gameplay concepts to engage users with signing in familiar scenarios.

The resulting uKinect sign-language e-learning games enabled these young people, along with their new non-signing colleagues, to learn workplace-specific sign vocabularies to help them transition from college to work environments. The games used an engaging animated avatar called Boris who demonstrated and responded to signs via an innovative Kinect sign-language recognition system. As well as being useful for these learners, the 'Boris Games' also demonstrated what was possible through sign-language recognition and won the TIGA Games Industry Award for Best Education Initiative in 2013.

Through the years, the innovations in response to the needs of these initial groups of people have enabled us to create similar breakthroughs for other groups.

Microsoft, whose Kinect was at the heart of the breakthrough in gesture recognition we created, put us in touch with the Guide Dogs charity that was looking for ways of making mobility training more fun for blind and partially sighted children. Working with a school for vision-impaired kids in

North London, we created the Nepalese Necklace games which took the body- and spatial-awareness exercises the kids had to get good at performing and made them controls for motivational 3D audio-games, turning 'boring' exercises into fun activities. The games transformed the kids' feelings towards their mobility training and improved their concentration on the rest of their schoolwork. They also won our team the Guide Dogs Partner of the Year award.

Microsoft also put us in touch with a hospital in Reading, UK that had been using Kinect games to help stroke patients' rehabilitation. The use of movement to control games was motivational for the patients, but the games' movements weren't the optimal ones recommended by their therapists and the games took too long to get started. We secured funding from Innovate UK to investigate whether gesture-based games created specifically to motivate stroke patients to repeat key exercises could drive their recovery of function without requiring occupational therapists and physiotherapists to constantly be present to guide and motivate them.

Over the course of the next six months we proved that we could do this, freeing up therapists to concentrate on higher levels of care for their patients, making more effective use of their valuable time. Our project was voted best presentation in its category at the Collaboration Nation event showcasing all projects Innovate UK funded in 2014.

Since then, Gamelab and Reflex Arc have taken the results of this innovation further into rehabilitation, adding virtual reality (VR) components and beyond.

As Richard England, Reflex Arc's CEO, says:

'When we started working with Hassell Inclusion to help students with communication difficulties, I never thought it would give me experience and skills that would help me create innovative mainstream VR experiences for the likes of Reebok. This is where thinking differently has got us. It's been quite some journey...'

This is just one example of a thriving sector of startups betting on innovation prompted by the needs of people with disabilities. Accessibility innovation is not just for the tech giants; it's for anyone with the imagination to make it happen.

You can find more details on this key in Chapter 7 of *Inclusive Design for Organisations* to gain inspiration and pointers to take your journey to the next level.

ISO 30071-1: your shortcut to accessibility maturity

'Do you want to avoid losing? Or do you want to win?'

'Embed it so that, like a stick of seaside rock, you can take a cross section of any aspect of your organisation and find the same values at play.'

'You need to fix the problem in the process not the product to prevent it reoccurring.'

'It's not the work you do; it's whether or not it helps people that matters.'

'This is where thinking differently has got us.'

These are the phrases that have steered me and my usability and accessibility team at the BBC, and then my team at Hassell Inclusion, all through the years since that radio show in 2008.

Three years later, my team and I had begun to put in place many of the things necessary to make sure our hard work at the BBC was really getting through to our users. More importantly, the British

Standards Institution had given me a chance to take that experience, enrich it by comparing it against what the heads of accessibility in other best-practice organisations had done and create BS 8878 to show others how they could do the same thing, and maybe win the awards we had won, providing organisational and process guidance to go with the technical requirements in WCAG. And eight years later, ISO has given me the chance to look at BS 8878 from the perspectives of experts in Austria, Canada, China, France, Germany, Holland, Japan, Korea, Spain, Sweden and the USA to deliver ISO 30071-1.

ISO 30071-1 is built on the combined experience of some of the world's most able accessibility experts – from those on my IST/45 committee at BSI, to those on international committee ISO/IEC JTC 1, Information technology, Subcommittee SC 35, User interfaces at ISO. It captures the progress in the accessibility journeys they've made so you can take a shortcut.

While BS 8878 provided advice on how to create or procure accessible websites and mobile apps, ISO 30071-1 extends this to digital products (or ICT systems, to use the language in the standard) used on a wider set of devices, including VR/augmented reality (AR) headsets, smart speakers, kiosks, in-flight and in-car entertainment systems, games consoles, automatic teller machines (ATMs) and electronic point of sales systems. It also considers the context of use of these products and what to do when the assistive technologies and accessibility guidelines that usually enable digital products to be accessible are not available on a device.

ISO 30071-1 has taken BS 8878's sixteen-step process for ensuring digital products are accessible when launched and maintained, and streamlined it into eight activities that can be integrated with whatever software development lifecycle methodology teams are using to create their products. ISO 30071-1 updates and clarifies BS 8878's advice on the relationship between inclusive design and user-personalised approaches to accessibility, including when to consider providing additional personalised accessibility provisions. It also updates the advice on business cases in BS 8878 to make it more appropriate for legislation and regulations in different countries which encourage or mandate accessibility.

It was launched in May 2019.

What digital products, hybrid products and ICT systems does ISO 30071-1 cover?

BS 8878 used the term 'web product' to denote the product being created. This was to make sure that people were aware that the standard applied:

- To different product types:

  - Intranet and extranet websites and workplace applications for staff, as well as external internet websites

  - 'Software as a service' cloud services (eg Google Docs), rich internet applications (eg Netflix), online games platforms (eg Club Penguin Online) as well as static information sites

  - Sites where content is created by users (eg social media, blogs and online encyclopaedias) as well as sites where content is created by the site owner (eg company information sites)

- On different delivery platforms and technologies:

  - Mobile websites and apps, as well as desktop websites

In ISO 30071-1 we extended the scope of the digital products the standard applies to, as our experience of using BS 8878 had indicated that its approach and harmonisation with non-digital inclusive design processes made it appropriate to extend to wider ICT systems and hybrid systems, such as:

- Social media

- Virtual assistants and chatbots

- VR/AR apps, and apps for smart speakers and kiosks

- Games on games consoles

- Apps for in-flights and in-car entertainment systems

- Software in ATMs and electronic point of sales systems

- ICT used in Internet of Things and smart cities

I've even used it to help an advertising agency think about the accessibility of motor show stands.

ISO 30071-1 uses the term 'ICT systems' to encompass this wider scope. But in this book, to ease understanding I'm going to use the more familiar term 'digital products'.

How this book expands on ISO 30071-1

This book is a guide to what's in ISO 30071-1 and includes the experience of my team at Hassell Inclusion of user testing its value (and BS 8878's before it) in the real world of digital product creation, not only in the UK but also internationally.

We've trained over fifty organisations in using BS 8878 to set their accessibility strategy in the nine years since its publication, and many of our insights from this experience have improved ISO 30071-1 to ensure it reflects the reality of digital production in 2019. We've also created tools and captured real-world examples to help people implement the standards in the culture of their organisation.

To illustrate many of the book's points and add real--world depth, I've included quotes from interviews I've conducted with some of the world's top accessibility minds on their areas of greatest expertise:

- Members of my team of experts at Hassell Inclusion on how people learn accessibility

- A United Nations (UN) agency director on how the rise of mobile devices has impacted accessibility

- Experts on understanding disabled and older people's use of digital products

- Experts in how to commission and carry out accessibility testing

- The creator of the accessibility ecosystem in Qatar

- People who've embedded accessibility in a Canadian bank, the Australian government, university document repositories and innovative e-learning games

In the support materials for this book, there are many such interviews, so I'd encourage you to register for them now to delve deeper into anything that particularly resonates with you as you make your journey.

I know that ISO 30071-1 can get you from the pain of confusion about accessibility to award-winning results because it's an expression of the journey that I, and many other accessibility experts, have gone on before you.

In this book's companion, *Inclusive Design for Organisations*, I detail how the first part of ISO 30071-1 helps make accessibility understandable and strategic by providing a framework to embed it within *an organisation*.

In this book we'll look at how the second part of ISO 30071-1 provides a way of embedding accessibility in your software development lifecycle to help turn it into a user-centred inclusive design process.

So let's dive in!

CHAPTER 2

Enable Process – How To Embed Accessibility In Your Digital Product Development Lifecycle Process

Let's be frank: for most organisations, accessibility isn't really embedded in their current digital development process. It's an addition tacked on at the end – if they're lucky.

While pretty much everyone in digital product development agrees that they should take accessibility into consideration right from the start when creating digital products, in most organisations this only extends as far as making sure designers and developers blindly follow WCAG in their work, and doing some accessibility testing to prove they've 'done it right' just before launch.

The problem is that this isn't working so well.

Why the current approach isn't working

There are numerous reasons that people have found the current approach isn't working:

- It doesn't allow you to validate accessibility requirements for how they will contribute to the levers of the product's success and growth (acquisition, activation, retention, referral and revenue[1]). Without this validation, sensible modern product management processes won't even allow accessibility requirements into the roadmap, let alone prioritise them against all the validated requirements.

- Different types of digital product may benefit from different approaches to accessibility, but the current approach doesn't take into account anything about the specific product you're making. The way to handle accessibility in a game app is different from the way to do it for a static information website for older people. Your approach needs to take differences between products into account, not ignore them.

- The current approach doesn't help when you're faced with any guideline that you feel isn't going to be appropriate or achievable for your product – you can't argue with WCAG, you're just supposed to conform to it.

- There's now more than one version of WCAG available for the web – WCAG 2.0 and 2.1 – so which should you pick? And other accessibility guidelines for creating mobile apps and other new digital product types (like wearables or games) exist. How do these relate to WCAG, and when should you use which?

- The current approach allows you to choose from WCAG's three levels of accessibility to aim for, but these are still crude devices for helping you quickly identify the highest priority accessibility requirements on projects with constrained budgets, resources and time.

- It doesn't tell you how best to test for accessibility, or when – when the design's ready, or a prototype's ready, or when it has been fully coded.

- It doesn't help when you've followed the guidelines, and yet your user testing has found that some people with disabilities still can't use what you've created.

- It misses out how to consider accessibility over the entire lifecycle of the product – from the original idea, through development, launch and post-launch versioning, to final decommissioning.

How ISO 30071-1 helps

The second part of ISO 30071-1 was designed to address all those issues. It identifies the key decisions made in product development that impact whether the product will include or exclude disabled and older people across the whole of its lifecycle, situates these as *activities* which you can integrate into your current process, and provides an *informed way of making these decisions* and *documenting them* to capture your best practice.

Embedding ISO 30071-1's activities in your current digital production process should improve it so you can reliably follow it to get accessibility 'right' for every different digital product you're creating. As Rob Wemyss – a member of our Hassell Inclusion team – said about using BS 8878 during his time as Head of Accessibility for Royal Mail Group in the UK:

> 'The standard has given us a framework to help reduce costs and improve our quality when delivering accessible digital products for our customers.'[2]

How ISO 30071-1's activities can improve your process

Let's start with the end in mind. I'd like you to consider what 'success' means with respect to accessibility for the product you are working on – what you'd actually like to have achieved at the end of the project in an ideal world.

I'm assuming you're not thinking of success as a one-off; you're thinking about success in the long term. Digital products these days go through different versions every day, so you need something that is continually successful; something that attracts huge numbers of users because it lets them do what they came to the product to do, and does it in a way that gives them all a good user experience; something that doesn't lose any of those users as it moves forwards, adding more content and functionality through new versions and redesigns.

ISO 30071-1's activities include the practices to put in place to *keep* your product successful, in terms of accessibility and other qualities, in the long term, as you *repeat* everything that's gone before to create new versions.

Obviously, you've got to start off with a version one, a great initial version of your product. How do you do that? You need to *do* – develop the product, making technical decisions every day on the specifics of how it should look and feel, how to code it, how to test it, how to decide when it's ready to launch.

This is the point where you'd be using WCAG, if the guidelines are appropriate for your product type and delivery platform. But you'd also need to know when and how it's best to test the product's accessibility; what to do in those situations where your gut is telling you that you need to break or modify the 'rules' for the good of the product; and what to do if you don't have the resource, budget or time to do everything 'best practice' and you can only prioritise the essential things.

You're going to need a firm basis on which to make your calls on prioritisation and rule-breaking. You'll want to be doing everything in a justifiable way, based on good strategic *decisions* that you've made before you start development: what the product needs to include; on what devices people will be able to use it; what level of accessibility experience you're going to aim to deliver, and for whom.

Finally, you'll need to base these decisions on solid *research*, because success comes from knowing what target audiences (if any) need your product; what your product needs to give them to satisfy their requirements; and understanding how people with disabilities will use your product, so you can understand how your following of accessibility guidelines will help them.

These are the four types of activity in ISO 30071-1. I call them the RuDDeR – *Research, Decide, Do, Repeat* – to keep you on course for success.

ISO 30071-1's activities are detailed in Part Two of this book.

If you integrate them all in your digital production process, by the time you arrive at the guidance set out by technical accessibility guidelines like WCAG, you'll already have gained a detailed understanding of the accessibility you want for your product and learnt how to make decisions based on justifiable reasoning. You'll be able to get the best out of WCAG, using it in an informed, pragmatic way, rather than as a straightjacket, because you'll already have established the strategic decisions you need to make about accessibility before going into the details of how you're going to deliver it.

How the activities align with user-centred design

ISO 30071-1's activities are based on best practice in embedding accessibility in digital product design used in creating some of the top websites and apps in the world, including my work at the BBC.

As digital products are often created to be used within non-digital contexts – think lift-control panels, ticketing machines or apps to guide people around theme parks – it is important that people creating these *hybrid systems* have ways of working that flow across non-digital and digital design. So the team creating ISO 30071-1 also worked to harmonise it with inclusive design and user-centred design processes for non-digital products.

To give you an example of this, in 2010–11 I represented the BBC as part of a European consortium of organisations exploring how to gain competitive advantage by making products inclusive, led by the Engineering Design Centre (EDC) at Cambridge University. Over the course of the year we proved that EDC's processes could be usefully applied across products ranging from confectionery wrappers to bank branches; from personal medical equipment to consumer white goods.

We also found that the processes, methodologies and tools that EDC had created – the Inclusive Design Toolkit[3] – related closely to much of what my team of digital usability and accessibility specialists were already doing at the BBC. What my colleagues on the programme couldn't understand was why accessibility guidelines in the web space were a technical *checklist*, when everything that they had learnt about inclusive design was about understanding user needs, encapsulating them in personas and using those personas to inform all stages of an iterative design *process*.

I used these insights to ensure that BS 8878's process for the production of digital products and ISO 30071-1's activities after that were designed to harmonise with non-digital inclusive design processes like EDC's, and with digital inclusive design processes like the ISO Standards for Human-Centred Design of Interactive Systems – ISO/FDIS 9241-210[4] – and inclusive design processes used by organisations like Microsoft.

ISO 30071-1's activities also include user-personalisation concepts that are unique to the adaptable, customisable nature of software. These add a useful flexibility to product development where the needs of one or more sets of users diverge from the needs of the majority of users.

How the activities align with business intelligence

Many people have noted that much of the guidance in BS 8878's steps and ISO 30071-1's activities reflects advice promoted by digital web experts from *outside* the accessibility field on how to build an effective website.[5]

Neil Collard, Strategy and Planning Director for e3, in his great seminar 'How shopping for shoes helped change the way we sell financial products'[6] says that to be effective, a website needs to:

- Be easily found by its target audiences

- Represent and develop your brand and its values online

- Maximise conversion (by ensuring all your visitors find what they need and become customers)

- Retain customers and drive value (by keeping the site fresh and responsive to the needs of your customers as your business grows)

ISO 30071-1's activities align well with this list, and its user-centred way of thinking about accessibility provides a great way of focusing digital product creation around these important things. ISO 30071-1 is based on a lot of business intelligence which, when followed, should deliver a *better* product, not just an *accessible* one. And this is slowly opening up organisations that have been resistant in the past to accessibility.

As Debra Ruh, CEO and Founder of Ruh Global Impact, USA, put it when I interviewed her:

'If we do not embed accessibility at the process level, we will keep trying but failing. However, if we encourage accessibility as part of the design process, we can be successful. Accessibility must be built into the development life cycle. We build privacy and security in at the process level, so should manage accessibility the same way.'

How to integrate ISO 30071-1's activities into your process

ISO 30071-1's activities do not require you to throw out your current digital development process. They are designed to be embedded within the existing process that you have, whether it's Agile or Waterfall, strict Scrum or bespoke.

This quote from my interview with Jennison Asuncion, talking about his time at the Royal Bank of Canada, gives you an idea about what it's like when you've successfully integrated the activities into your process:

> 'What's neat about the standard that you built, and why I was happy to get on board, is that you understood that accessibility is more than just the guidelines. Naturally and necessarily there's a wrapper around the guidelines. The wrapper can include who's responsible for what. What about the people with disabilities? What do we need to think about for them?

> 'You're actually talking about the processes that are necessary to execute accessibility and achieve value from people's best efforts. People need to know to include accessibility

in testing, so that means QA. They need to include accessibility in the design, so that means the business systems people and the UI designers. They need to know to budget for it, so that means the project manager has to play their role.

'The project manager also has to schedule the time for the testing. Maybe adding extra time in development if a widget needs to have more time spent on it to be made accessible. So that's how all the different roles fit in – the responsibilities end up naturally having accessibility pieces because we're baked into the process.'

Integrating ISO 30071-1's activities into your development process may initially seem daunting, but over the last eight years my team has done this with organisations large and small; with multinational corporations consisting of large numbers of geographically dispersed siloed production teams and external suppliers, and digital agencies with a staff of two; with long-established companies using well-embedded production processes, and startups with no written production process at all. ISO 30071-1's activities are flexible enough to fit within the structure of your process or design framework – whether it's Waterfall or a flavour of Agile. They fit well, for example, in the BBC's published Product Lifecycle Management process.[7]

To embed the activities in your existing process, I recommend you:

1. Review your existing development process to work out where each of the ISO 30071-1 activities would most naturally fit. This will get you to an updated 'first cut' process for your organisation.

2. Test out your updated process on one non-mission-critical development project to check its fit with your company's culture and products.

3. Analyse how well the updated process supported you in delivering the desired level of accessibility in the product.

4. Make any tweaks to the process to optimise its fit with your culture.

5. Create a case study about anything that was useful, if you have time.

6. If the process brought benefits to the project, create a plan to roll it out to your other digital product development projects and monitor its impact there.

To embed the activities in smaller organisations without a process, I recommend you:

1. Follow the ISO 30071-1 activities I'll detail in the following chapters in order – their order is designed to align to the Human-Centred Design Process in ISO 9241-220, so you'll effectively be walking through that process

2. Adopt anything that works for you

How ISO 30071-1 helps you make justifiable decisions

Another essential aspect of ISO 30071-1's contribution to accessibility best practice is its requirement for organisations to make decisions in each activity in a way that is informed, justifiable and transparent.

A huge number of decisions are made across the team of people working on a digital product every day. While ISO 30071-1's activities highlight the *key* decisions made in digital production projects that have most impact on accessibility, all decisions, to a greater or lesser extent, may have an impact. So it's important for each member of the digital production team to be *empowered* to make decisions, to know how to make them *well*, and to know when they should ask for decision *support* from accessibility specialists.

This may seem like teaching your grandmother to suck eggs, but my team has found that it's essential grounding for understanding how to get the best out of ISO 30071-1's activities. It replaces the rigidity of most accessibility guidelines with permission for team members to use their brains in working out how to make a good decision in the context they're in.

ISO 30071-1 encourages team members to be aware that every decision should:

- Be recognised as a decision

- Have all options and their implications considered

- Be made based on justifiable reasoning

- Be noted in the product's 'ICT system accessibility log' for transparency

And it requires team members to do this for each one of its activities.

This is essentially a democratic, empowering way of working. It encourages team members to think carefully about why they are about to do the things they are about to do, whether there is another way of doing things and what the implications are of each. It encourages them to make decisions based on their own understanding of the product and the best available research on its users' needs in the country or culture in which they will be using it.

Fundamentally, it places accessibility back in the sphere of cost benefits like all other decisions made on a project. Understanding that accessibility isn't the only important quality that teams are trying to embed in their product, it enables team members to 'listen to their gut' in dealing with situations where blindly following accessibility guidelines may feel like 'the tail wagging the dog' when the amount of work necessary to make some functionality work for a particular group of disabled people is overwhelming the rest of the work on the project. It also handles situations where fully complying with a set of technical accessibility guidelines is actually infeasible or unreasonable for a particular digital product.

As an example of the importance of this thinking, consider the accessibility of YouTube. The purpose of YouTube is to allow the general public to upload their own videos to share them with anyone who would want to watch them. Two aspects of this purpose provide real challenges to making it conform to WCAG AA.

For a video to be fully accessible, it needs to include captions, audio-description (AD) and interpretation into sign language, but as it is unlikely that users will include such access services with the videos that they upload, video on YouTube can only be made accessible by YouTube itself. But the massive amount of video being uploaded to YouTube every minute of every day makes it both technically infeasible and economically unreasonable for YouTube to be required to provide access services for all of its video.

To give a benchmark comparison, the BBC's 'gold standard' commitment is to provide AD on 20% of all its broadcast programming, achieving almost 30% of programmes on iPlayer with AD in 2018.[8] And yet, for YouTube to reach WCAG AA it would need to audio describe 100% of its videos. That makes no commercial sense.

The important thing here is the competence to be able to justify your decisions and the discipline to always write that reasoning down.

As Brian Kelly, Director of UK Web Focus, put it when I interviewed him on the importance of being able to bring these practical business decisions into accessibility compliance in the education sector:

'What we're talking about is really a user-centred approach to providing services. What we're saying is you look at the users and you look at their requirements and the challenges in providing these. The difficulty we have is a set of technical guidelines that are great and over time they've evolved, but unfortunately, they've been treated as if they've been enshrined in legislation: "We feel we have to do this."

'Suddenly the user isn't there any longer. It's not about the user. Strict conformance with treating those guidelines as mandatory requirements means services are lost.

'Within a university context, imagine all of those peer-reviewed papers in institutional repositories which are in PDF format and typically do not have alt-tags in their images. What should you do? Do you help to enrich the accessibility of those resources by removing them? That's quite clearly preposterous.'

This lack of understanding of the challenges and costs of accessibility in guidelines and by legislators was perfectly demonstrated in 2017 when the University of California Berkley cut off public access to tens of thousands of video lectures and podcasts in response to a US Justice Department order that it make the educational content accessible to people with disabilities.[9]

While the University said it has plans to create new public content that is accessible to listeners or viewers with disabilities, content that was inaccessible to people with disabilities is now inaccessible to all. That is equality, but I don't think it's a solution to anyone's needs.

How to document your decisions

ISO 30071-1 requires you to record these justifiable decisions in a document called an *ICT system accessibility log*. This document is an active log for internal use into which each accessibility decision made over a digital product's lifecycle (after launch as well as before launch) is detailed.

This is useful for five reasons.

Firstly, the ICT system accessibility log is like the Captain's Log in *Star Trek*. You know the drill: Captain Kirk talks into his Captain's Log before going down to the surface of the planet, most likely to find some sort of crystal that the Enterprise needs to continue 'boldly going where no one has gone before'. He takes down two red-shirted men to the surface of the planet alongside more recognisable crew members. And anyone who's seen the programme knows what regularly happens: when they beam back onto the ship, the two red-shirted men have not made it.

My ideal James T Kirk at this point goes back into his cabin, listens to the reasons for going to the planet surface that he dictated into his Captain's Log and considers whether the expedition was worth losing two members of his crew for. The Captain's Log enables him to revisit the reasons behind his decisions after he has got a better understanding of the implications of those decisions.

Being a captain is not easy, and part of the job is to make complex decisions based on incomplete knowledge of what the consequences will be. But a good captain improves the odds in the long term by using their log to learn from their mistakes, whether they were hot-headed, ill-judged, naive or unavoidable.

The same reflective learning is possible, and the maturity of an organisation's approach to accessibility can be easily examined, by reviewing the decisions in its ICT system accessibility logs. This is what 'Iteration is used to progressively eliminate uncertainty during the development of ICT systems' in clause 7.1 of ISO 30071-1 means.

While ISO 30071-1 does not place such an emphasis on conformance as technical accessibility standards like WCAG, it requires organisations wishing to claim conformity with ISO 30071-1 to make their ICT system accessibility logs available for inspection to provide evidence of how they've followed the recommendations and guidance in the standard.

Secondly, the ICT system accessibility log is like a 'black box' flight recorder. If the worst-case scenario happens and the plane goes down, crash investigators always look for the black box because it contains a recording of the decisions made on the flight-deck in the vital last few minutes before the crash happened. Most of the breakthroughs in flight safety have come from analyses of such recordings – read Malcolm Gladwell's fabulous *Outliers* book to see him prove that.[10]

The worst-case scenario for digital accessibility is complaints from users that turn litigious. Here,

ISO 30071-1's concept of 'justifiable reasoning' links with the concept of 'reasonableness' that is part of many nations' disability discrimination laws, such as the 'reasonable adjustments' required in the UK Equality Act 2010 and the phrase 'reasonable accommodation' which is included as a general principle under the Americans with Disabilities Act.[11]

Lawyers on BS 8878's writing team who originally came up with the idea considered the link between its principle of 'justifiable reasoning' and 'reasonableness' to be sound, and following ISO 30071-1's advice in noting the justification for your decisions may help present a case for 'reasonableness' if you need it in legal proceedings, but until case law is established that tests the link, the two terms cannot be considered to be analogous.

More concretely, my experience in dealing with accessibility complaints is that most disabled people dislike product owners' failure to consider accessibility much more than being given a reason why the accessibility feature they needed wasn't included, even if they disagree with that reason.

Thirdly, the ICT system accessibility log is useful while the project is running as it allows the team – especially its product manager – to keep track of the research conducted and accessibility decisions made on the project. The product manager needs to be able to review quickly whether decisions being made are sensible and justifiable, not just individually (does the decision chime with the accessibility goals of the product?), but also cumulatively (does it make sense in the context of other decisions already made?). They need to be able to see any relationships between decisions – how one decision has prompted others, or where a decision has been made that undercuts previous decisions (for example, where a project has already created or procured a media player that can play captioned video, but then a decision is made to not caption any of the video being delivered by the project). They need to be able to quickly review how each decision impacts the whole project's level of cost, benefits and accessibility risk, as this is the key way of assessing the justification of each decision, and track the *accessibility risk profile* of the product as it evolves.

Fourthly, the ICT system accessibility log is essential where you are outsourcing or procuring the product externally. It becomes the set of written accessibility requirements that you need to place in your invitation to tender (ITT) or request for proposals (RFP) document to ensure potential suppliers know what you expect. It gives you something to measure suppliers' tenders against when making procurement decisions, as it requires suppliers to say how they will do accessibility on *your* project, rather than allowing them to trot out the 'right answer', which most know is 'WCAG 2.0 AA', without understanding what that means for your project. And it is a great help if suppliers or product vendors cannot deliver all of your accessibility requirements and you need to prioritise them to meet project budgets.

Rarely does a product come to market that is perfectly accessible – these are the realities of modern product development. The ICT system accessibility log will detail all those pragmatic decisions made where the constraints of budget, resource or launch date have justifiably overridden the risk of not making all aspects of the product accessible.

The fifth use of the ICT system accessibility log is in helping to create the *ICT system accessibility statement* for the product, which you publish as part of the product to inform its users of the reasoning behind decisions you have made that may detrimentally or positively impact their ability to use it. ISO 30071-1's Activity 7 details how to create this accessibility statement.

NOW IT'S YOUR TURN

- To get the most out of the rest of the book, I'd encourage you to think of one particular product that you're involved with and how you'd complete each activity for that product. It can be any digital product, whether you're just starting out on its creation, or are already at version five; whether the product is one in a large portfolio that you oversee, the single product that you own, or you're one part of the team creating the product for a product manager.

- Download a copy of the ICT system accessibility log template from the book's follow-up materials, if you haven't done so already, and fill it in for your product in the 'Now it's your turn' sections in each activity. That way you'll be building a useful record of your thinking as you work through the activities, capturing your initial thoughts on the product, its context of use and its audiences' needs, and using these to inform you in making each decision later in the process as you aim to balance costs with benefits and accessibility risk.

- If you have the time, integrate the questions in the template into your existing project documentation system to embed the activities into your team's culture of decision making, making it your business as usual.

- Where you find you have more questions than answers in applying insights from an activity to your product, write the questions down and take them to your product team to engage them with your thinking. As Hassell Inclusion workshops have found, in many organisations, it's this sort of practical real-world discussion that has the greatest impact on product teams and the accessibility of the products they are creating.

PART TWO

THE ACTIVITIES

ACTIVITY 1

Specify The Widest Range Of Potential Users

A s your digital product's accessibility strategy is going to depend on its purpose and audiences, you need to think about those audiences and what they want from your product right from the start. Then you can use this information to inform your strategic and technical decisions when you are creating the product.

Time spent getting this established now will pay off in spades later on, as this research will ensure that your decisions aren't based on wrong assumptions that might fail to connect your product with its target audiences. You need to define:

- Who your product's target audiences are

- Whether you will treat your users as individuals or groups of users

a. Define your product's target audiences

Your audiences are the people who will make your digital product successful, or not. They are your most important stakeholders, and your only way of managing them is to understand their needs and preferences – and find some way of meeting them through your product.

That's a tall order if you're trying to do everything for everyone.

Trying to be all things to all people can cause you to fail to do anything well for anyone. And as most coaches will tell you, it's best to find your niche and devote yourself to serving the people in it. It's likely that your digital product won't have universal appeal but will appeal to a certain set of people who are interested in what it is all about – its purpose (that's Activity 2).

Unfortunately, in their rush to enable universal accessibility, most guidelines fail to acknowledge that not all digital products are intended for all audiences. But knowing who your digital product is and isn't for is essential to make sure that the accessibility decisions you make in its creation are right for those users. That's why ISO 30071-1's activities start by defining the product's target audiences. The key distinction, which fundamentally impacts on accessibility, is whether the purpose of your digital product is designed:

- To appeal to everyone (or at least a range of audiences)

- To appeal to a particular part of a public audience

- For a restricted and known audience whose access you can predict or control

Designed to appeal to everyone

At one extreme are digital products that are intended to be used by the widest range of audiences. You might be creating a website for a Google, a BBC or an Amazon.

This is the biggest challenge for accessibility as you will need to design for the widest possible audience, and may not be able to find out any information about your users other than through the use of analytics or sign-on mechanisms that encourage them to give you this information for a more personal user experience (see the second part of this activity).

Designed to appeal to a particular audience

If your digital product is public-facing, it may still be designed to appeal to a particular part of the public audience. It may be for older people (so called 'silver surfers'); it may be to help young children with their learning; it may be for people living in your town; it may even be designed specifically to support a particular group of people with disabilities.

All of those things are fine. It is OK for you to design a product for a particular audience.

Being clear on who your target audiences are can enable you to make decisions to optimise the user experience of your product for their needs and preferences, and target the accessibility decisions you make. For example, knowing whether you have a wide or a narrow target audience is essential to understanding how to apply accessibility guidelines on the use of plain language – how to write for the reading age of your audience and the vocabulary you can assume they will have. If you're creating a site whose purpose is to teach people how to understand Shakespeare, it's likely to be for a wider audience than a site for Shakespeare scholars, so the level of language you'll need to use will be different.

Designed for a restricted and known audience

At the other extreme from products designed to appeal to everyone, your digital product may be designed for a restricted audience whose access to the product you are completely in control of. If it's an intranet or extranet, or even a client area of your public website, you can predict and control who will use it because every single user must be logged in to gain access to it. No one will be using your site unless they have signed up, answered whatever questions you require for access, and logged in, so you know exactly who is using the site at any time.

That information can be exceptionally useful to help you minimise the cost of unnecessary accessibility work. If you have no current staff with learning difficulties, it is much easier to make a case for the reasonableness of not doing everything you can to make sure your intranet gives an optimal user experience to people with that disability. Of course, the situation will change if you recruit someone with that disability and retro-fitting accessibility for them will be more costly than building it in from the start, but de-prioritising that aspect of accessibility until that point seems reasonable if you do not have the resources to do it earlier.

Similarly, if you are providing the assistive technologies that your staff members who have disabilities will use to access your intranet, you only need to ensure that the site is accessible using those assistive technologies. This removes the requirement to give users an accessible experience on all the alternative assistive technologies they could have chosen (see Activity 3).

Enabling the digital product to know who is using it because they're logged in also presents the opportunity to give them a user experience that is tailored to their individual accessibility needs (see the second part of this activity).

Primary and secondary target audiences

Once you've specified your target audiences, it's useful to *segment* them into groups with similar needs from the product in terms of key goals and contexts of use. A simple way of doing this is to define *primary* and *secondary* target audiences for your product based on the people you believe will be interested in it and with an idea of what they'll come to your product to find.

For example, the *primary audience* for a restaurant website would be people who want to decide whether to eat there or in a competitor's restaurant. They are the people you need to give the right messages (information and feel) to so they'll do the 'call to action' you want, which is to book a table.

Secondary audiences might include people who are interested in a more general way, for example about the restaurants in an area that they are thinking of moving to. These audiences may bring you custom in the future, but appealing to your primary audience could affect your bottom line right now.

So what's all this got to do with inclusion and accessibility?

Accessibility is all about another *dimension* to those audiences – whether some groups of people in your target audiences have particular needs, perspectives and capabilities that should impact how you create your product. While it makes sense to focus your product on people with particular interests, it also makes sense to appeal to as many people with those interests as you can, unless there's a good reason not to.

To continue the restaurant example, you'd choose to focus on serving food that is on your menu rather than anything people might want to order, but if the costs weren't prohibitive, you'd aim to serve that menu to as many people as you can, even if it meant redesigning the layout of your premises rather than blocking some people from becoming paying customers.

Similarly, on your restaurant website, you'd look at what might block people from becoming customers. For example, you'd consider providing information on how people who use wheelchairs will be able to get into your restaurant and use its facilities. If you don't have this information on your site, they may go elsewhere. And if vision-impaired people can find enough information on your site to decide to visit, but can't book a table due to accessibility limitations in the technology you use for handling online bookings, you've lost another group of customers.

Ensuring that as many people as possible in your primary and secondary audiences can use your product, whatever their abilities or disabilities, is a great way of maximising your customer base. That's what inclusive design is all about, and it is what ISO 30071-1 requires – specifying the product's groups of intended users to include the widest range of potential users.

Trade-offs and conflicting needs

That said, it's worth remembering 'reasonableness'. It's not possible to create a digital product that includes everybody – 'universal design' is an ideal, not something that is actually deliverable. Rather, the art of inclusion is to balance that ideal situation with what's practical.

On every digital product I've worked on, there have been times when the product team hasn't been able to create something which will appeal to all the audiences they've wanted. UX designers are usually up to the challenge of designing website navigation to meet slight variations in the user goals of target audiences, but it can sometimes be impossible to cater for everyone's needs as people with different types of disability can have contradictory needs to each other and those without disabilities. And sometimes the costs of catering for the needs of one disabled group can be prohibitively high.

To give an example from the world of e-learning, many people, including those with learning and literacy difficulties, might learn best about sustainability by playing a game where they can see the environmental impact of the choices they make, but as games are visual and highly interactive, this choice might make it impossible for a person who is blind to access the learning without a huge amount of extra work and expense. While user-personalised approaches can help go beyond 'design for all' to 'design for me' – see the second part of this activity – if you have the time and resource to include them, for most products, you're likely to have to make trade-offs between whose needs you are going to concentrate on catering for, and whose you are not. It's best to acknowledge early on that you are likely to need to make these trade-offs over the course of the creation of your digital product and to establish a way to do this that is justifiable. And your justifications must depend on cold, hard facts as the basis on which to make decisions.

That's why, while I believe that there are few good reasons to justifiably say that your website 'isn't for disabled people', it makes perfect sense to look further into *how many* people with different types of disability or who are older will be likely to use your site and what their needs and preferences are. This is what we'll look at next.

NOW IT'S YOUR TURN

Use the questions in the ICT system accessibility log template to guide you in thinking about who your product's primary and secondary audiences are.

b. Understanding disabled user groups

This second part of Activity 1 is essential to ensure that you are not making any false assumptions about how your users will use your product. Get this wrong and you may create a product that people don't want, people can't use, requires assistive technologies they don't have or doesn't make sense in the context in which they wish to use it. Get this right and you have a chance that your product will be a lucrative success.

What do you know about your digital product's target audiences? About how they use the web and what they might want from your product? Are they like you or completely different? It's a good idea to spend time and effort working that out before you start creating something for them, because if you don't understand the users you are creating the product for, even if you create a usable product, it may not be one they actually want.

> 'By far the most common mistake startups
> make is to solve problems no one has.'
> — Y Combinator co-founder Paul Graham[1]

Your product may be a solution to a problem your target audiences don't have. Or it may be a solution to a problem they do have but that doesn't fit into their lifestyle. And you really don't want to find that out when you user-test the product two weeks from launch, when it's too late and costly to do much about it.

That's why ISO 30071-1 advises you do some *user research* early to find out more about your audiences. It's about making sure you don't base decisions on assumptions that may not be true. It's about letting your audiences help you decide what the product should be, so when you user-test it later, it really connects with them, delights them and keeps them coming back for more.

Three aspects of user research that you need to know to delight your audiences

It's time to look deeper at who your primary and secondary audiences are, and what they may need from your product.

It's useful to break this down into three aspects:

1. How many people are we talking about in each target audience, and does each audience have subgroups within it (for instance people with different types of disability)?

2. What are each audience's *general* needs from the user experience of *any* digital product, and are there subgroups who have different needs from each other?

3. What are their specific needs from *your* product?

The first of these aspects is essentially quantitative – all about numbers. The second and third are qualitative – about more detailed characteristics and opinions. But for each, you effectively have two different ways of finding out the information you need, depending on the resources you have available to you:

- Do some general desk research, collating information that is already available freely to the public or can be bought from research agencies

- Commission or conduct your own user research

We'll look at the second and third aspects in Activities 2 and 3. Here we'll focus on the numbers.

Finding the number of people in your potential target audiences

Finding good research on how many people are in your primary and secondary audiences is essential. If you don't know this:

- How do you know whether or not the audience is big enough to warrant the time and money you'd need to invest to create a product for them?

- How do you know how much of your total potential audience your product is appealing to when you review your usage statistics after launch?

Here's an example from my time at the BBC. BBC iPlayer was one of the first video-on-demand (VOD) services in the world. Its purpose is to enable online audiences to catch up on TV and radio programmes they may have missed. This makes the primary audience for the service pretty much everyone in the UK who is online, as almost everyone watches BBC TV.

As 90% of households are now online (2018 figures for the UK[2]), the BBC's huge investment in iPlayer makes good sense. And the result is an impressive monthly performance: 356 million TV and radio programmes were watched and listened to in January 2019.[3]

While the BBC does not publish unique user figures, it does publicise its demographics and has noted for some time that usage 'remains predominantly under-fifty-five years in terms of age'. This is 'in line with home broadband users', but is still 'younger than the typical TV viewer's profile'. So even though the BBC has worked to extend access to the service from web to a huge number of devices including mobile and digital TV, it could potentially attract many more users (especially older ones) if it found new ways of encouraging people to get online.

You may not be the BBC and may not have a product that everyone wants to use, but the same principles apply – find out as much as you can about the potential size of your audience and use that information to inform how much to invest in your product and to monitor how well you are doing compared to how well you could be doing. If you are reaching 10% of your potential audience, you've got lots of work to do. If you're reaching 90%, growth is going to be hard, but you may need to ensure no competitor is about to steal your audience.

While there are many sources of statistics available on general use of the internet, if your product is a website the cheapest and easiest way of estimating its potential audience size is to use Google AdWords Keyword Planner[4] to see if anyone is searching for keywords related to what your website aims to deliver – its purpose. This also tells you which words people are using for their searches so you can put those words in your site's titles and headings to attract the audience. More information on this is available in any number of SEO blogs.[5]

What proportion of your potential target audience may be disabled or older people?

What about those who are disabled or older? How much of your potential target audience might these subgroups make up? Is your audience likely to be experiencing the multiple minor impairments of ageing?

Ferraris now have doors that are easier to get into for older people – because Ferrari worked out that most of the people who could afford one of its cars were ageing. And it's why the page on cold weather payments on a government website should probably pay more attention to the needs of older people than a site promoting holidays in Ibiza.

It makes perfect sense to look further into *how many* people with different types of disability or who are older will be likely to use your site. If these numbers are high, make sure these audiences (like all your others) get hooked on your site's user experience. If these numbers are low, the benefit you could gain from spending time and money appealing to these audiences may not give you a good ROI, unless that investment is also low.

Finding reliable ways of sourcing these figures is challenging. If you are redesigning an existing site, you could count the number of people visiting any pages of your site that are targeted at disabled people – your accessibility statement, for example. Unfortunately, this really only counts the number of disabled people using your site who find problems with it (see Activity 7 for the reasons why).

Even though web analytics systems can now tell you how many male or female users you have, they cannot tell you how many disabled people are using your site. To provide some help, my team are creating a cloud-based accessibility personalisation tool that can inject some of this information into a site's analytics when users specify their look and feel preferences for the site, so its owners can track the size and activity of some anonymised disabled audiences on the site (see Activity 5).

Where these 'actual use' analytics are not available, the information you have to go on is the best figures you can find of your 'potential accessibility audience':

- The population of people with various types of disability

- How many of those people in general are using the internet

The total accessibility audience and how it breaks down into different groups

The best figures I've been able to find of the potential disabled audience in the UK are:

- Total population of the UK: 66.9 million (2019 figures from Worldometers, which has stats for most countries[6])

- Total disabled people in the UK: 13.9 million (2017 figures from the 'Family Resources Survey Report 2016/17'[7]) – that's 22% of the population in 2017, up from 19% in 2014

It's worth finding these figures for every country your product is likely to be used in. Disability figures may not be so readily or reliably available for every country – there are parts of the world where disability is unfortunately still seen as something to be hidden, either by the disabled person themselves, or their immediate family, so censuses will tend to under-report the number of people with disabilities.

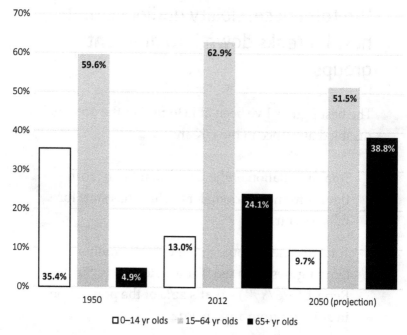

*The impact of population ageing: changes in the population of Japan
(Source: Japan Statistics Bureau, MIC, Ministry of Health, Labour and Welfare)*

On top of this, the statistics on population ageing
are startling. At present about 18% of the UK's
population are likely to have a combination of minor
impairments due to ageing rather than disability.[8]
Every month more than a quarter of a million
Americans turn sixty-five.[9] And the population
forecasts from Japan for 2050 predict a massive
ongoing demographic change (as shown in the figure
above):

- In 1950, over-sixty-five-year-olds made up 4.9% of the population

- By 2012, this percentage had risen to 24.1%

- Projections for 2050 indicate this figure will reach almost 39%

Knowing the *prevalence* of different impairments in disabled and older audiences can also be useful later for understanding how many people may benefit from you following accessibility guidelines designed to help a particular impairment group or groups. Different organisations will quote you different numbers for this (I use a combination of figures from disability organisations and estimates from the 'Family Resources Survey Report 2016/17'[10]), but these are a reasonable approximation:

- Almost 11 million people in the UK have a hearing impairment which is disruptive to their lifestyle, of which 24,000 use British Sign Language to communicate[11]

- Approximately 6.3 million people are dyslexic; one in six adults has the reading level of an eleven-year-old[12]

- About 4 million have difficulties using their hands which may impact their use of computer keyboards and mice[13]

- About 3.5 million have a mental-health condition[14]

- About 2.4 million people have difficulty with memory or concentration[15]

- About 2 million have a learning difficulty[16]

- Almost 2 million people have a vision impairment which is disruptive to their lifestyle, ranging from those who may have difficulty reading text without it being enlarged through to those who may need to zoom the display of their computer up to sixteen or thirty-two times, and 360,000 are registered severely sight impaired (blind)[17]

- About 1 million children and young people have some form of communication difficulty[18]

- About 700,000 people are on the autism spectrum[19]

- About 150,000 people have a progressive, cyclical or fluctuating condition such as multiple sclerosis[20]

- And almost 75% of disabled people have more than one of these impairments[21]

The relative size of each audience may be a real surprise to you. Often people's assumption is that accessibility is just about people who are blind, due to the success of their lobby in getting their needs known, but they only make up around 2.5% of the current disabled population.

While it can be true that making your website work well for people with one impairment tends to help those with other impairments too, this isn't always the case. To give one example: making your site work well for 360,000 people who are blind will do little to help almost 8 million people who can see your site but need the colours changed for comfortable reading because they are dyslexic or have lower-level vision impairments.

As Sarah Lewthwaite, Research Associate in Education at King's College, London, said in my interview with her:

> 'WCAG tends to be very keen on text and text-based representations of information for screen reader users. Providing captions for video and that kind of accessibility work can be expensive and time-consuming. Practically, that means to hit particular accessibility checkpoints, people just don't use video. But more globally, literacy levels and other factors may mean that people would prefer video to text-based alternatives.

'I think that's one of those spaces where we can see that WCAG as a set of guidelines creates a hierarchy of impairment. It's important for us as accessibility practitioners to recognise how particular disabilities are conceived of, grouped, and then hierarchised within standards. Where BS 8878 and ISO 30071-1 have a strength is that you can understand and look at the hierarchies that may be in play and address them, whereas somebody who is stuck, potentially, with a checklist just isn't going to have that space to re-represent under-represented groups.'

I'll come back to these people's needs in the third part of this activity where I'll talk about personalisation.

The impact of age on impairment

If your digital product is for a primary audience of older people, or children and teenagers, it's important to realise that these figures may also change with age, as the prevalence of some impairments is impacted by age, while others are not.

To give an example, the UK's statistics for prevalence of disability in children of school age[22] (gathered as part of the 'statementing' process that children go through to be recognised as having special educational needs) are at large variance with the statistics for the adult population. Children are less likely to have vision impairments or hearing impairments, and are much more likely to have learning difficulties, dyslexia, behavioural or social difficulties, or communication difficulties.

The lower figures for vision and hearing impairments make sense as these impairments tend to develop or worsen as people grow older. The figures for learning difficulties and dyslexia show how society and education are growing in understanding of these particular conditions and disabilities. A dyslexic child in the education system thirty years ago may not have been picked up as dyslexic and may still be covering up this aspect of themselves as an adult. This is less likely these days.

Conversely, the multiple minor impairments of ageing tend to be hearing, vision, dexterity or memory-related.

Demographically, what are disabled people like?

- Disabled people are more likely to be older – 70% of disabled people in the UK are over the age of fifty[23] compared to 40% of the general population.[24]

- Disabled people are more than twice as likely to be unemployed as non-disabled people.[25] They are less likely to be people's colleagues at work. They are less likely to eat in restaurants or go to cinemas or theatres than non-disabled people, because of their lower incomes and the fact that life costs you £570 more on average per month if you're disabled.[26] This helps to explain the lack of visibility of disabled people to the rest of the population.

- Research that I commissioned at the BBC found that disabled people tend to be heavy media consumers, particularly of TV and radio, possibly because they are likely to spend more time at home than non-disabled people.

- Whatever the official disability definition states, only half see themselves as 'disabled'. The name of their particular disability is something that they would relate to, but the label 'disabled' is not one that all would own.

Disabled and older people's use of the internet – an improving statistic

There is one last statistic which you may think would constrain the value of the time you put into making your products include disabled and older audiences: the number of people in these audiences who currently use the internet.

In the past, disabled people's use of the internet was low – figures in 2010 found that only 41% used the internet.[27] The figures in 2018 were up to 80% with 'little difference in recent internet use between disabled and non-disabled adults in the sixteen to twenty-four age group'.[28] While this is still 11.5% behind usage by people without disabilities, the figures are encouraging. Similar increases in older people's use of the internet – rising from 19.9% of people aged seventy-five and over in 2011 to 43.6% in 2018 – are also encouraging.[29]

The reasons these figures are encouraging is because people with disabilities and those who are ageing have as much, if not more, to benefit from the internet than the general population. To give one example, people with physical or vision impairments are likely to benefit from shopping via websites rather than having to travel to shops on the high street.

To understand why the figures aren't higher, and what is being done about it, we'll need to dig deeper. In Activity 2, we'll look into qualitative research of disabled and older people's use of the internet – what they feel about the experiences they get and whether they'd want to repeat them.

NOW IT'S YOUR TURN

- Check out the size of the potential audience who may be interested in your site with Google AdWords Keyword Planner.[30]

- Think further about whether disabled and older people will be interested in your digital product and note down the size of the audience you might be excluding if you don't cater for these subgroups' needs. This 'size of excluded audience' is a great way of putting together a business case for work you may want to consider doing to prevent their exclusion in later activities. Check out EDC's handy exclusion calculator for a visual way of working out these figures.[31] This is a great addition to the documentation you'll be building up for your product from each ISO 30071-1 activity.

c. Define the relationship the product will have with its audiences

One big complication for the creation of successful digital products is that your user groups may have different or even contradictory needs. The third part of this activity asks you to consider whether your product should include the one facility that may enable you to make it more accessible to many of your users – the ability to personalise it to their needs.

This is all about expectation management; about understanding that defining the relationship your product has with its audiences is vital to giving them a great user experience.

The ease with which an ICT system can include personalisation to an individual user's accessibility needs, and the likelihood that the user would expect the system to offer such personalisation, is impacted by whether the product considers users to be individuals or general members of a group of users:

- **Products that consider users to be general members of a group** assume that their relationship with their audience should be one to many. Their owners will make their one product work for as many of its users as possible by ensuring there are ways for them all to do the thing they came to it to do. They may provide user journeys optimised for different groups of users (as captured in user personas – see Activity 3) but never for an individual user.

An example of this would be the BBC CBeebies Playtime app[32] that my son loved when he was little. The main user journeys in the app are all games for its primary audience – children from around two to six – to enjoy. But there's also a subtle 'grown-ups' button in the app that takes parents – the app's secondary audience – into a different set of user journeys, allowing them to learn how the games can help their child's education and how to maximise their child's learning by playing along with them.

- **Products that consider users to be individuals** are ones that require or encourage you to create a login. Some sites and apps would be of no use without a login. On Twitter, you would have to follow everyone in the world and tweet anonymously. It would be a free-for-all of people sharing information with everyone else with no filter mechanism, which would ruin its purpose – Twitter wouldn't be Twitter.

Other products may be useful without a login, but the login improves the experience by providing users with a personalised interface. BBC iPlayer has a 'favourites' option to specify the programmes you like so you can find them as easily as the editorial choices the BBC suggests you watch. You allow the product to know who you are and track your usage, as long as the product will use its knowledge about you to give you a better experience.

While this distinction was maybe a little ahead of its time when BS 8878 launched in 2010, these days almost every website you visit or app you download encourages you to identify yourself, whether it's registering to receive a newsletter, subscribing to get full access to articles, or just confirming that you're happy to receive a site's cookies to comply with cookie legislation. Look at the text of most cookie consent banners and you'll see some variation on 'we use cookies to tailor your experience, measure site performance and present relevant offers and advertisements'.

'Tailoring your experience' raises the user's expectations. If a product can support my 'wants' (for example, an email app allowing me to choose a coloured theme so its navigation controls reflect my personality), then why shouldn't I expect it to

support my 'needs' – the things that I absolutely
have to personalise so I can use it at all (like
changing the colours of emails because I can't read
text in the default colours the designer or author
chose)?

It is interesting that most current websites that
include personalisation functionality focus it on
'wants' not 'needs'. Yet if you think of Maslow's
famous hierarchy of needs,[33] 'needs' are much more
fundamental to a person's well-being than 'wants'.
If I can't use the site comfortably, then it doesn't
matter if it responds to my preferences around
recommendation. It first needs to respond to my
preferences about how comfortable it is for me to use.

In Activity 5 we're going to look at how digital
products can use personalisation mechanisms to
enable people with different types of accessibility
preferences to get a user experience that meets
more of their needs. For now, it's important to note
that if your site or app has a login mechanism and
encourages the user to expect a personalised one-
to-one experience, those with impairments may be
more likely to expect you to give them an experience
which is personalised to their accessibility needs
as well as their wants. Moreover, having already
gained the user's buy-in for personalisation, you
will find it easier to convince them that the product

can be *trusted* to give them a more accessible user experience if they disclose their personal access needs.

NOW IT'S YOUR TURN

Use the questions in the ICT system accessibility log template to note whether your product considers users to be individuals or general members of a group. You will need this information later in Activity 5.

ACTIVITY 2

Specify User Goals
And Tasks

N ow we've defined the product's target audiences, we move on to looking at the purpose of the product (the tasks users are going to come to the product to achieve), the context of use of the product (the situations in which they are going to use it) and how these will impact your accessibility strategy for the product.

You need to specify:

- The purpose of the product

- Its user goals and tasks, and which are core and non-core

- Any constraints which the context of use places on users' ability to use their preferred technologies (especially assistive technologies)

We will cover these three things in Activity 2.

a. Specify the purpose of the product

Although people say, 'Think about accessibility from the start of your product creation', this is something they often forget. But doing this can immediately highlight many of the key accessibility challenges they'll face. There's one thing that changes least about a product during its creation but impacts its accessibility the most.

I'm talking about specifying the *purpose* of the digital product and using this to anticipate the biggest challenges to making it accessible.

The accessibility challenges inherent in products with different purposes

While the W3C Web Accessibility Initiative (WAI) team that maintains WCAG intend the guidelines to address all types of web technology – all good standards try to cover the future, as ISO 30071-1 does – WCAG 2.0 was written in a pre-social-media, pre-mobile-apps, pre-responsive-design world. It was an easier time to create digital products that were accessible. While WCAG 2.1 has brought WCAG more up to date, most organisations are still using WCAG 2.0 without realising it's ten years old.

That is not the world we live in any more. Digital products now have much wider purposes than the web of ten years ago. They've moved from:

- 'The web as information' to 'the web as video portal, games portal, software as a service, window on interactive experiences'

- 'The web as information to be consumed' to 'the web as a place to create my own content'

- 'The web' to 'digital' as users have become used to reaching for an app on whatever device they have with them to find information from the internet, rather than solely using a website on a browser on a computer

- Moreover, digital products are replacing increasing numbers of older non-digital service channels, as customer service becomes digital through 'digital transformation'.

Each of these wider purposes brings with it significant challenges for accessibility. I would argue it is as essential for the YouTube or Facebook app to be accessible as your local council's information website. And try telling my nine-year-old son that games aren't an important part of the internet. So it's essential to note the purpose of your digital product immediately and check to see if any aspect of that purpose is going to have big implications for the decisions you'll need to make around accessibility.

I'll use three different product types to illustrate how important it is to consider the purpose of your digital product right from the start.

Wikipedia's purpose poses an interesting question for accessibility. The purpose of Wikipedia is to allow people to create and share an encyclopaedia of knowledge collaboratively online. There's one aspect to that purpose that will immediately be key to the accessibility of the product: the people who own the website – Wikipedia – do not create the content on it; their users do. So the key question has to be: whose responsibility is it to make sure that the content is accessible?

It will be a real challenge for Wikipedia to keep its website accessible, unless it can ensure its content authoring system enables users to create accessible content and persuades them to take the responsibility, or Wikipedia commits to editing user content to add accessibility itself with an army of moderators. That has big intellectual property and copyright implications, as well as resourcing implications for Wikipedia.

We've already touched on the similar challenges of making YouTube accessible, which are even greater than Wikipedia's. Its purpose is to allow people to upload and share video with everyone else. It will not be feasible for the site to be fully WCAG 2.0 AA compliant, unless YouTube can create systems that automatically generate captions and AD for every second of video that its potentially unlimited number of users upload. YouTube and many others are making steady progress with improving the quality of their automated captions creation, but even if they manage to reach 99% accuracy, the concept of getting a computer to watch a silent video and automatically create an AD for it is a far-off dream, if it's possible at all.

Now let's look at internet-only banks. Their purpose is to allow people to do their banking in a more 'modern' way without the need for branches or call centres.

The accessibility of these banks' websites and mobile apps is critical. Customers of traditional banks could use branches or call centres to check balances, make transactions and manage their money, if they couldn't use the website or app. The safety net of these alternative customer-service channels has been removed for online banks, so customer expectations of the accessibility of the digital products is high. And these expectations will be the same whenever a digital service completely replaces an existing non-digital customer service (for example, a phone helpline) for any organisation.

Finally, many products may not be able to be made fully accessible due to a clash between their purpose and the capabilities of a particular disabled user group. Can 3D experiential games really be made accessible for people who are blind, or an e-learning module on melody for people who are deaf?

You need to know the purpose of your digital product right from the start of its creation as its purpose will fundamentally impact its accessibility strategy.

NOW IT'S YOUR TURN

Use the ICT system accessibility log template to guide you through noting your product's purpose and any immediate accessibility implications arising from it.

b. Split the product's user goals and tasks into core and non-core

If you don't have the time or resource to make every part of your product accessible, what should you do? The second part of Activity 2 gives you a strategic way of prioritising accessibility work so you can best handle that circumstance during development.

After specifying the product's purpose, you need to specify the user goals and tasks it will support. This will undoubtedly be part of any digital production process your organisation already has – specifying the 'user journeys' your target audiences will expect your product to provide is the heart of the requirements gathering that a business analyst completes before the product can be built.

If the purpose is one sentence that summarises the whole product, this is where you delve deeper; where you consider:

- What goals your audiences are going to come to your product to achieve

- Whether there is any hierarchy in the goals, where one goal needs to be accomplished before another is possible or makes sense

- Whether all your target audiences will want to achieve the same goals, or whether some goals are more important to some audiences than others

Differentiating core and non-core goals to facilitate prioritisation

One of the key contributions of ISO 30071-1 to making accessibility practical is the recognition that you may not be able to do everything for everyone all of the time. There are trade-offs in the process of creating products, and that applies to accessibility as much as any other aspect of the product, so you need to be sure of what the priorities are for the accessibility work that you do. If there is only a limited time that you can spend on making sure the product is accessible, on which parts should you prioritise your time?

The important thing for accessibility here – from the perspective of the impact on your audiences rather than protecting yourself from risk of litigation – is to support *complete* user journeys. It doesn't make sense for you to have made one part of a user journey fully accessible if the other parts of the journey exclude people. For success, your users need to be able to get all the way from the first step of the journey to the last, as Jennison Asuncion highlights in my interview with him:

> 'Here's an experience I had a number of years ago. There was an airline in Canada where I was able to create my reservation and all of that stuff. The last step, I submitted my credit card number and I'm like, "This is perfect. I'm about to go."

> 'But before I could do that, I had to solve a CAPTCHA [a completely automated public Turing test to tell computers and humans apart]. Of course, at that time we didn't have audio CAPTCHAs. I'd gone through steps one through seven before that eighth step – I'd already spent twenty minutes on the other steps, because the site itself wasn't that accessible. So I'd made my way all the way through, and then suddenly a barrier came up and bit me in the ankle. I couldn't

do anything. I had to bucket out and call a sighted friend to do the process for me.

'So when suppliers ask me, "You have X number of WCAG things that you want us to satisfy. Can you prioritise which ones we do first?" I don't like to tell them, "These are the priority guidelines to do first." I would rather say, "These are the priority transactions or screen flows to do first. Fix them completely." Because if you end up in a situation where they're going to say, "OK, we'll work on these guidelines first, and then these other guidelines next", what you end up having is an inconsistently accessible experience. I'd rather have a fully accessible experience on five screens than an inconsistent experience across thirty.'

It's also important to define what goals are *core* to your product and what goals are *non-core*, based on your understanding of what your users want from the product.

For example, on a VOD service, being able to find and play a programme is core. If you can't do that, the whole purpose of the product fails. Being able to rate that programme and share it with your friends is not core. Those goals are useful – many people want to share their experiences with technology, and it may help the VOD service owner if you spread the word about their great content – but if the content itself isn't accessible, how can you tell anybody how good it is? All you could really say is that you couldn't watch it. And that's not the sort of thing VOD services want you to share with your friends.

I'll give you another example from the cloud-based accessibility personalisation tool my team is creating. Its purpose is 'to allow website owners to add a tool easily to their sites that enables disabled and elderly people to get a more accessible user experience by allowing them to specify their preferences about how the site should look and function, and getting the tool to alter the site to correspond to those preferences'.

Our user research found that many people who could benefit from accessibility personalisation tools didn't use them because the tools didn't support their particular needs, or took so long to show them the benefits that they gave up before finishing the process of specifying their needs. So the core goal of the product is to quickly and vividly give users an understanding of how it could change a site to better suit their needs by getting them to an initial set of preferences which our research found helped many people with their particular disability. Once this has gained their attention and trust, the non-core goal is to allow them to further customise that starter theme to more precisely suit their needs.

These examples illustrate the difference between core and non-core goals – if you can't make the core goals accessible, it doesn't matter how accessible the non-core goals are as people will already have been excluded (or will exclude themselves) from getting the real value of the product. So, if you have a set amount of time to spend to make sure accessibility is considered on your project, prioritise full user journeys for core goals over anything else.

NOW IT'S YOUR TURN

Use the ICT system accessibility log template to guide you through documenting your product's user goals, splitting them into core and non-core

c. Understanding how disabled people use digital products

The other essential aspect of your product to consider for accessibility is the context in which people will use it – the devices they'll be able to access it on and the environments they will do that in. For you to understand the importance of this, you need to first understand how disabled people use digital products.

What are your *general audiences'* needs from the user experience of *any* digital product?

There are research agencies all over the world that can help you do qualitative user research into the needs and preferences of your users. Most of them are incredibly good at what they do, having evolved ways of working that go beyond asking people what they *think* they want from digital products to observing them using products in the course of their day to see what they *really* do with them. Unfortunately, their services are often costly, so how are you going to research these needs without breaking the bank?

A great start is to find freely published research into how people use digital products that user-research agencies share to promote their more bespoke services. Google any of these agencies and you're likely to get some useful free insights: Amberlight, Clearleft, cxpartners, Gartner, Nielsen Norman Group, Nomensa, System Concepts, User Vision, Webcredible, What People Want Agency. Any of these companies will tell you how people are using digital technologies at the moment, as well as what their general needs are for a website or app to meet:

- Their desire to be both satisfied and delighted by the user experience

- Their need to access the product's services across the variety of different devices they use in many different contexts of use

The days are gone when you could assume that your users would be sitting at a desk, whether at home or in an office, when using your product. You can no longer assume they will be using a computer with a certain amount of processing power and a large screen. And you can't assume that the environment in which they use your product is static and quiet, or that they will be completely focused on your product when using it.

One of the reasons why accessibility is getting more and more important every year is because we are all 'blind' in relation to the screen when we are driving a car – we should not take our eyes off the road or we might crash. We are all hard of hearing when we are in a noisy environment and are trying to listen to the audio of a breaking news video. We are all motor impaired when our iPhone is buzzing in our pocket when we are jogging.

All of these aspects of the *context* in which people use devices feed more and more into the idea that impairments are not just experienced by people with disabilities – we are all impaired in some senses at different times. And because we cannot assume that people have all of their abilities available to them when they are using a website or mobile app, if we think about people who are impaired due to a disability, it can help us understand how everybody may use our products when they are 'temporarily impaired' because they are doing something else at the same time.

What are your *disabled audiences'* general needs from the user experience of *any* digital product?

You can find background information on disabled people's use of digital products from the following sources:

- The WAI document 'How People with Disabilities Use the Web: Overview'[1] can provide a good grounding in the sorts of experiences different groups of disabled people get from digital products, and the accessibility preferences and assistive technologies they use to optimise their experience with those products

- If you prefer to consume information via video, case studies of the way people with disabilities use assistive technologies can be found on My Web My Way[2] or by searching for 'disabled access to digital' on YouTube

You can find more up-to-date research on disabled people's use of digital products on sites like WebAIM[3] (whose yearly Screen Reader Survey[4] is exceptionally useful), gov.uk[5] (whose Assistive Technology Survey 2016[6] enriched WebAIM's survey by looking at other assistive technologies as well as screen readers) and the Hassell Inclusion blog[7] where my team regularly share our latest user-research insights.

To summarise, the important thing to know about how disabled people will use your product is that their user experience will be mediated by a number of technology layers that your digital product sits on, where accessibility facilitators (settings and preferences) can transform it, if you have coded it correctly to accessibility guidelines, to better meet the needs of the user. This I term the *accessibility ecosystem*, and it is key to understanding how accessibility strategies need to flex depending on the type of product you are creating, the devices it will support and the context of its use. I will introduce the accessibility ecosystem here and refer back to it over the next few activities.

Introduction to the accessibility ecosystem

The accessibility ecosystem has ten levels, from your digital product at the top down to the user at the bottom. Together they make up the context of use of your product. At each level, it may have accessibility facilitators like settings or components.

- At level 1 is your *digital product.* This includes websites and apps. Accessibility facilitators here include in-product accessibility personalisation options, such as 'style switchers' to allow the user to resize text and change colours.

- Below that, at level 2 are the *implementation technologies* that your product was created with. These include technologies to build websites and hybrid apps, like HTML 5, CSS 3, JavaScript and WAI-ARIA; and technologies to build native apps, like Swift and Java. Accessibility facilitators here include accessible native elements (like HTML5's input type='date' date picker); and accessibility APIs (like iOS's UIAccessibility methods).

- Below that, at level 3 are any *enabling technologies* that you used to speed up your product's development. These include frameworks and libraries like React JS, Angular JS, Cordova and PhoneGap; and content management systems (CMSes) like Drupal, WordPress, Adobe Experience Manager and Sitecore. Accessibility facilitators here include accessible themes, plugins and components.

- Below that, at level 4 is the *browser* the user will access your product through if it is a website. This includes Internet Explorer, Edge, Chrome, Firefox, Safari, Opera and UC Browser (used a lot in China) in mobile and desktop versions. Accessibility facilitators here include support for new HTML 5 native elements[8] and WAI-ARIA; browser accessibility settings (eg text size); and browser extensions/toolbars (eg to change colours). Note: for apps, this browser level is missed out of the ecosystem.

- Below that, at level 5 are any *software assistive technologies* that are installed on to the device. These include JAWS, NVDA, ZoomText, Dragon, Eye Gaze. Accessibility facilitators here include settings to customise the assistive technology to the user's preferences (eg speed of screen-reader voice).

- Below that, at level 6 is the device's *operating system (OS)*. This includes Windows, MacOS, iOS, Android and bespoke kiosk or ATM OSes. Accessibility facilitators here include OS accessibility settings and in-built assistive technologies like VoiceOver and TalkBack, Google Voice Access and Apple Voice Control (the variety and quality of these will depend on the OS version).

- Below that, at level 7 are *hardware assistive technologies* that may be attached to the device. These include specialist keyboards, trackballs, various types of switches and Braille displays. Different devices will support different hardware assistive technologies. For example, all of these technologies can interface with smartphones, none can interface with in-flight entertainment screens, but many can interface with the Xbox games console via the Xbox Adaptive Controller.[9]

- Below that, at level 8 is the *device* that the product is being used on. This includes smartphones, tablets, desktop/laptop computers, eBook readers, smart watches, smart glasses and AR/VR headsets, games consoles, ATMs, kiosks, in-flight or in-car entertainment, and digital user interfaces (UIs) that are installed in buildings (eg lift controls, lighting panels, room-booking screens).

- Below that, at level 9 is the *physical and social environment* the user is using the device in, including:

  – The social environment – whether the user's experience of the product is personal (on their own device, privately); shared over time (on their own, but on a shared device such as a hot-desk PC or ATM); or shared at the same time (with other people on an interactive screen in a museum or big screen at an event).

  – The physical environment – location, including: at home; while travelling; in the office/school.

  – The physical environment – approachability. A product is considered to be approachable if diverse people can overcome any physical or psychological barriers and physically or remotely access it to accomplish tasks. Factors include:

    › Reachability: for example, whether sufficient space is provided in front of an ATM for a person using a wheelchair to get into position to use it

› Privacy: for example, whether blind users feel assured that their personal identification number (PIN) won't be easily viewable by other people behind them in queues at ATMs and electric funds transfer at point of sale (EFTPOS) terminals

- Finally, at the bottom level, level 10, is the *user*. Users may have varied levels of familiarity and confidence in using digital technologies and products, and varied levels of awareness of all the facilitators in the accessibility ecosystem that they could use to give themselves the most accessible experience of your product.

Now you know how people with disabilities use digital products, the other things to find out are:

- Whether disabled people in your target audiences are likely to have any preferences for using one type of device or another – for example, if you're creating a website, whether they'd prefer to view it on a computer, tablet or smartphone

- Whether there is anything about the context of use of your product that will place any restrictions on them being able to use it

NOW IT'S YOUR TURN

Take time to familiarise yourself with the basics of how disabled people use digital products using various elements of the accessibility ecosystem by watching the video case studies in My Web My Way.[10]

d. Noting the technology preferences and restrictions of the product's target audiences

The standard way of delivering an accessible user experience requires *you* to create your product to comply with accessibility guidelines like WCAG and *your users* to have the computer, tablet or smartphone they use your product on set up with the assistive technologies and accessibility preferences to handle their particular needs, as per the accessibility ecosystem. This part of Activity 2 is all about checking during your user research if there is any reason that your users won't be able to live up to their end of the bargain, and what you should do about it if that's the case.

You'll hopefully recall my example from Chapter 2 of the blind pensioner who wrote to me complaining that I had incorrectly assumed that people like him would have the latest version of the JAWS screen reader, when in reality it was too expensive for him to buy. This is just one example of a *technology restriction* that the standard way of doing accessibility doesn't handle well.

The question is: for your product, is it safe to assume that you can rely on the user to choose the right browser accessibility settings (for example, a person who is dyslexic choosing a setting which changes your site's colours to a more soothing colour scheme for readability) or install the right assistive technology (for example, a person who has a severe vision impairment using a screen reader to transform your site into spoken text) to iron out the differences between their needs and everybody else's?

Ideally, the user's accessibility settings or assistive technology provide all of those transformations for you, so all you have to do is to code your product to ensure they happen correctly. When that's working well, accessibility is a shared responsibility between your users and your product. But what happens if some people in your target audiences don't have the spending power to buy or confidence to install the assistive technologies they need? In that situation, should you go to greater lengths than you usually would and design the product to do some of the transformations itself?

Activity 6 addresses that issue head on: whether you'll need to provide 'additional accessibility measures' – tools embedded in your product that, in and of themselves, remove the need for the user to install assistive technologies to give them a good user experience. But you can only make decisions in that activity if you've noted down any technology preferences or restrictions you find during your initial user research that indicate you need to consider additional measures.

These are the types of preferences or restrictions to look out for and note when you're doing any user research:

Preference: for mobile due to cost of technology

On top of the issues around the cost of screen readers for older people, it could be that the user has a strong preference for mobile due to concerns about cost.

A Pew Research Center Study in the autumn of 2016[11] found that:

'57% (up from 41% in 2012) of adults with a
disability have broadband at home compared
with 76% (up from 69% in 2012) of those
without a disability... [but] groups that
have traditionally been on the other side of
the digital divide in basic internet access –
especially those in lower-income households –
are [now] using wireless connections as their
main way of getting online.'

Other research has found that many low-income
families most often use a smartphone or tablet for
internet access.[12] As people with disabilities are less
likely to be working than the rest of the population
(see Activity 1), it is also likely that many get online
via mobile devices.

So people who argue that it's only necessary to make
desktop websites accessible are completely missing
the transformation in access to the internet that has
already happened. It's entirely possible that if you
have to choose only one device on which to make
your products accessible because you don't have
time to do everything, the best place to spend your
accessibility time and money is on mobile, not on
desktop. This sort of counter-orthodox finding is
often something that only user research can reliably
tell you.

Preference: for smart watches

Anecdotal research has indicated that some people on the autism spectrum prefer to use smart watches rather than smartphones, as 'knowing I have a form of communication strapped to me is a hugely reassuring thing'.[13]

Restriction and preference: due to fear

Older people are often scared to download and install new technologies onto their computers due to stories of friends getting viruses or people getting access to their personal information via phishing emails. That means that while it's possible and free for them to add a toolbar into their browser to give them easier control of the text size of websites, they are unlikely to do so. And due to their understanding that tablets are less vulnerable to viruses, they also tend to prefer tablets to desktop or laptop computers.

Restriction: due to ignorance of accessibility settings and assistive technologies

It is also not always the case that you can assume that people with disabilities know about the existence of accessibility settings and assistive technologies that have been created to meet their needs.

Research that I did in the noughties indicated clearly that many fewer people were using assistive technologies than would benefit from them. Microsoft research from 2004[14] had found 57% of American computer users between eighteen and sixty-four years old were likely to benefit from accessible technology. Yet what I found in the UK was that only about 6 to 8% of web users use some form of assistive technology or accessibility preferences in their OS or browser.

This prompted me to commission the creation of My Web My Way at the BBC to help educate people on the possibilities of assistive technologies. It was considered a big success when it was launched in 2006, but still didn't quite make the impact that I wanted.

Here's what my collaborator David Banes, former Chief Executive MADA, Qatar, said when I interviewed him about it a few years later:

> 'In all my experience across the years, the biggest barrier to accessibility is awareness: enabling people to find the products that

are available; the services that are available; the information sources. Naming things is so important... What is it people will search for to find this information? What is it that they think they're looking for and how do we match it to that expectation?

'We won awards together for My Web My Way, and it was great that the site used video as an accessibility aid to learning as we knew some of the site's audience would have difficulty reading text. But people could only find it on the BBC site if they clicked on the "accessibility" link. And we didn't do the PR to enable them to know what that word meant. Something that had so much potential was actually being used more by people like you and me to train accessibility experts in understanding the range of assistive technologies than the people who would actually benefit from those technologies.'

Thankfully, awareness has improved since then with assistive technologies becoming a standard part of the OS of most smartphones, and being promoted in Apple WWDC sessions[15] and by Microsoft in Sunday newspaper supplements in the UK.[16] But I'm hoping organisations putting accessibility options in the standard setup wizard of new devices will bring an increase in the number of people using accessible technology who could benefit from it.

Microsoft has been doing this for years in Windows setup. And Apple from iOS 13[17] has included accessibility in the turn-on settings of its devices. For a generation of people like my mum who would benefit from something as simple as knowing they can increase text size on their emails, this could be a game-changer. This could also help awareness of people in Third World countries who don't have the support of disability organisations or Apple Stores to let them know what their smartphones can do to better suit their needs (see my blog 'Accessibility in Developing Countries – Insights from Ethiopia' for more details [18]).

Restriction: due to complexity

Some assistive technologies, especially screen readers, are complex bits of software that require training to learn, so young children may not have the cognitive ability and older people may not have the confidence and motivation to learn how to use them.

Restriction: due to local IT policy restrictions

People could be stuck with old technology if there are IT policy restrictions in place on the devices on which they use digital products. Often IT support policies prevent users from being able to change settings to prevent them from changing those they shouldn't. But these restrictions often also prevent users in offices, libraries or internet cafés from being able to set accessibility preferences in the browser or OS, or install the assistive technologies they need.

This research around preferences and restrictions will be invaluable in ensuring the decisions you make in later activities will enable disabled people to get a good user experience of your product alongside everyone else. Relying on disabled people to have the technology to give them that experience may not always be a sensible idea. While it may save you from legal risk, it may deprive you from gaining their custom.

e. The impact of the device(s) that your product will support

'In the past few years, we have seen more mainstream accessibility features in mobile products than in the entire history of IT before. For the first time, major vendors are competing for accessibility, because accessibility features on mobile devices in general are useful to everyone, not only persons with disabilities. So you have scale.

'For instance, if you're in a country or region where it's not authorised or permitted to use your phone when you're driving, you need to be able to activate your phone by voice, you need to do everything without touching your phone. That is effective for a person who is paraplegic. You could be trying to read a text message in a sunny place, so you can't see your screen. Well, text to speech becomes a good tool for you. So how about that for blind persons? When SMS started to expand quickly, it became the preferred vehicle for deaf persons to communicate between themselves, with their parents and friends.

'Mobile technology is always there, in your pocket, in your hand; you can carry it; it's available all the time. GPS can tell you your geographic position and you have near field communication to activate stuff in your home. It's unbelievable.

'And now look at wearable devices, the glasses, the watches, maybe some implant sometime. So you can think about a number of new services, and we do that at the M-Enabling Summit once a year in Washington with all the mobile industry. The number of inventions, innovations, apps and services that people create with those new tools is mind-boggling.'

That's what Axel Leblois, President and Executive Director at G3ict – The Global Initiative for Inclusive ICTs – said to me when I interviewed him back in 2014.

Mobile has changed the way we use the internet rapidly. And other new device categories with internet capability are piling in after that.

Mary Meeker's million-viewed SlideShare 'Internet Trends 2019'[19] reveals that while digital media usage has remained fairly stable for the last ten years, daily hours spent with digital media on mobile by adults in the USA grew from 0.3 hours in 2008 to 3.6 hours in 2018. Daily mobile usage is now almost 1.5 times desktop/laptop usage.

Mobile has also changed accessibility massively. Axel Leblois's quote shows the opportunities mobile presents for disabled people.

You've already seen that smartphones, tablets and smart watches are the preferred devices for many disabled and older people. Axel's quote also highlights the way mobile has widened the 'audience for accessibility' because we may *all* benefit from accessibility features as solutions to the 'temporary situational impairments' that we experience due to the different *contexts* in which we use mobile sites and apps.

I used my Mac's high contrast mode to combat the bleaching effect of the sun on my laptop screen when I wrote some of this book on the beach on holiday. When the environment you're in is noisy, captions will help you understand the YouTube video you're trying to watch, just as the captions on TVs in bars enable customers who want to catch up on news to do so without disturbing others who just want a quiet drink with friends. And Apple obviously agrees with the ideas on accessibility features helping everyone consume web content safely while driving. Apple CarPlay[20] is partly based around Siri's voice detection so you can interact with your phone without touching it (which was initially designed for people with motor impairments), and VoiceOver text-to-speech means content can be read to you as well as read on screen (which was initially designed for blind people).

Mobile as a model for the impact of new delivery platforms on digital product strategy

While mobile is still the current focus for much discussion around accessibility, digital products are also being viewed on an increasing plethora of devices, not just desktop and mobile.

New device categories are growing rapidly. The Amazon Echo has now been purchased by 47 million people in the USA, doubling its user figures every year. Wearables like the Apple Watch are taking longer to establish, doubling their user figures in four years, but have now been purchased by 52 million people in the USA.[21]

TV-on-demand sites, like BBC iPlayer, Netflix and Amazon Prime, are well established, with American people watching 28% of their TV online. No wonder that Disney Plus and Apple TV+ will be launching in Autumn 2019. Programmes can already be viewed on everything from traditional desktop computers, laptops, tablets and smartphones, to games consoles, connected smart TVs and TV set-top boxes.

There are new technologies coming onto the market all the time – whether they're a completely new device category, browser or version of a browser, or a new implementation technology to create digital products in. There are always at least two or three 'next big things', some of which will actually turn out to be the future of the internet, others of which will fail and become footnotes in technology history.

In 2010, when we created BS 8878, my committee took a punt that we needed to help organisations think about how to do accessibility on mobile and connected TV. Now, nine years later, mobile support is a no brainer – hardly anyone makes a product that isn't responsively designed to work well on mobile, and the question is often whether your mobile app should be *hybrid* or *native* rather than whether you should develop a mobile app version of your product at all.

And after a slower start, connected TV has become important. Most new TVs and set-top boxes have wifi and access to streaming services via apps, and the likes of Apple TV are leapfrogging more established set-top boxes by including assistive technologies like VoiceOver as standard.

As mobile has become established, we're looking forward at wearables such as smart glasses, smart watches and VR headsets, and uses of mobile devices to control ever more aspects of our environment through Internet of Things APIs (see Activity 5). And, as the range of devices for which to create digital products expands, so does the range of purposes of digital products. This is why the scope of ISO 30071-1 includes many device categories.

How to decide which devices to support

Most people are used to reviewing the devices that they have with them and choosing to view the content they wish to consume on the one that makes most sense for the type of content in the context they're in. I'll check my bank balance on my mobile, research mortgage deals on my tablet and apply for the best one on my laptop. Our digital user journeys may start and end on different devices, but we want the user experience to be consistent, and consistently good, all the way through the journey.

While there are many device categories that you *could* support, the number of permutations is likely to have a considerable impact on the budget and timescales needed to deliver your digital product. As the languages used to create native apps are different between mobile OSes, such as iOS and Android, and the number of screen sizes of smartphones and tablets on each OS proliferate, mobile will also tend to complicate some of your technology and design choices.

The range of devices that you could support may change over time, but the way of thinking about them strategically remains the same. To decide whether to support a device, product managers consider:

- The benefits of supporting it: the size of its installed user base and what the device and OS will allow the product to do (specific functionality that other OSes do not have that fits the product proposition well)

- The costs of supporting it: how easy it is to create products for the device

In this context, the desire to create products that are inclusive is a complicating factor. Often product managers *hope* that their mobile sites will be accessible if their desktop sites are. This may not be the case as the support for accessibility on different mobile OSes varies widely, as does the take-up of devices on those OSes by different groups of disabled people.

If you do not consider these issues when making your decisions on which devices and OSes to support before starting development, you may find yourself unable to implement your products to be as accessible as you're aiming for. So how should accessibility impact your device support decisions in terms of which OSes you create apps for and which devices you optimise your website's user experience for? And how much should your product adapt to the challenges and opportunities of each device and OS to give all your users a great user experience in the context in which they will use your products?

How accessibility impacts which devices to support

Are you in control or is the user?

The first question you need to answer in deciding which devices to support is whether you have any *control* over the devices on which your users access your digital product.

For any publicly available digital product that people will consume through a browser, the user has the control. This is why browser-based solutions to providing a *consistent quality* of user experience over a diversity of devices are essential, as we'll discuss in the next section. The only control you have is how far to take these approaches.

When it comes to apps, you have complete control. You can choose to create an app for a particular device's OS and make it available via the device's app store, or you can choose not to.

What's popular in general and with disabled audiences?

While you are looking at the installed user base for a device category, it's worth looking into how many people with different disabilities are using it. Research has found that these figures may be different from the general population and are almost always linked with how well the OS supports accessibility. If a technology doesn't support the needs of a particular group of disabled people, they won't adopt it.

To give an example, while figures for the *global* take-up of Android are higher than iOS,[22] WebAIM's annual survey found that 22% of *screen reader users* use Android devices, whereas 75% use higher-priced iOS devices (with the remaining 3% using other platforms).[23] This is despite vision-impaired people being less likely to be working than the general population.

What's interesting is that this is not because Android doesn't include a screen reader – its TalkBack is not noticeably inferior to Apple's VoiceOver [24] – but Apple has made it much easier for blind and partially sighted people to choose to buy their products. All Apple products include VoiceOver as standard, and have done for years, whereas Android's more complex value chain obscures its messaging to these audiences – Android was late to the party, and while TalkBack should now be on all Android phones, people get confused with the differences between phones from different Android licensees. Even for people who have less money than the general population, it makes more sense to buy a phone that they know *will* work for them rather than a cheaper phone that *might*.

What opportunities will the device's accessibility support provide?

While many people focus on the *challenges* of making mobile apps accessible, it's worth lingering for a moment on some of the features that make mobile, and other devices like smart speakers, such an *opportunity* for disabled and older people.

Firstly, assistive technologies that you might have to buy, or at least install, on a PC frequently come as standard on mobile devices. The huge variety of sensors included in the smartphone or tablet device may also be used in your product to help the user – it knows where you are via satellite GPS and what you're near via near-field communication; it knows how you're holding it and the ambient light where you are; it knows personal things like your heart rate and what your calendar says you should be doing at the moment.

For example, while 'use my location' is a convenient time saver for many people, it could be the difference between a blind person, or a person with severe motor impairments who has difficulty typing their location into a box, being able to use 'store finder' functionality comfortably or not.

Moreover, mobile apps that provide personalised accessible remote controls to a variety of inaccessible real-world objects are potentially a breakthrough solution to give many disabled people easier control over the environment around them. Examples of this control include:

- The use of smart speakers like the Amazon Echo or Google Home to control household objects – for example, televisions,[25] central heating controllers[26] and lights[27]

- The use of mobile devices and 'movie reading' apps to give people personal AD of movies in cinemas[28]

- The use of e-readers to give museum visitors personal accessible electronic guides to exhibitions as they walk around the gallery[29]

We will discuss further examples in Activity 5.

What challenges will the device's accessibility support cause?

For most organisations, the key accessibility consideration is *how easy* it will be to make websites and apps accessible on the device. Challenges here include:

- The impact of differences in screen size – for people with low vision, small screens can be problematic, whereas for blind people the size of the screen is completely irrelevant as they don't use it anyway.

- The impact of differences in input device – for people who have motor difficulties, touch screens can be much harder to use than physical buttons or tactile keyboards, and multi-finger gestures can be a complete barrier.

- The impact of mobile browsers and OSes omitting standard accessibility features, such as the ability for the user to override text and background colours or change the size of text on a website through the browser. To get around this, as we will discuss in Activity 5, you may need to provide these as 'additional accessibility measures' in your product.

HTML-based hybrid apps offer the promise of the same sort of cross-OS portability that HTML enables for websites, but many organisations choose to develop native apps for each OS as they allow apps to make full use of the specific functionality in the device.

For native apps, you have the challenge of the different programming languages and accessibility

APIs you need to master to make apps accessible on different OSes. Your ability to make apps accessible will depend on the quality of the accessibility APIs the OS provides. While the accessibility APIs of most modern OSes are increasingly comprehensive, this does not hold for all of them.

The situation is also changing over time, so check out the accessibility documentation of each OS you are considering supporting[30] to see if it will allow you to deliver to your accessibility aims. Check to see whether each OS's app store has an accessibility rating system, or even if it requires apps to be accessible to allow them onto the store. (Advocates for people who are blind and vision impaired are debating how to encourage Apple and Google to change their stores to require app accessibility.[31])

The decision to 'go native' will obviously impact your choice of guidelines to direct accessible production. The more OSes you support, the more sets of OS-specific guidelines your developers will need to master. And while all follow the *spirit* of WCAG, notably its perceivable, operable, understandable, robust (POUR) principles (see Activity 4), the implementation techniques and the way they are structured will be different for each OS.

Designing your product to provide an accessible user experience across different devices

How much should your product's design adapt to the challenges and opportunities of each different device to give all your users an appropriate user experience in the context in which they use your product? ISO 30071-1 advises that you have two options:

1. **Responsive design.** You could create one accessible product, with a responsive design, and ensure that you test its accessibility on desktop and other devices.

2. **Adaptive design.** You could create multiple product versions (sites and apps) that each include an appropriate UI and functionality subset that is appropriate for the device and context in which your product is likely to be used on the device, and fully test the accessibility of each version.

The benefits of *responsive design* are already obvious to anyone who has used a responsive site. 'Nobody likes horizontal scrolling' and 'no one wants to read tiny text' are pretty much 'Usability 101'. Who wouldn't want a site to rearrange its layout to fit the size of the device's screen so no horizontal scrolling or zooming in and out of the screen is necessary?

What's maybe not so well known is that responsive design actually has its roots in accessibility. Early experiences of using mobile devices' small screens as windows on to a larger website were similar to the experience screen magnifier users have had on computers for years. Responsive design is really an updated name for the 'liquid design' or 'text reflow' solutions to these users' difficulties that accessibility advocates were promoting many years in advance of mobile browsers presenting everyone else with the same difficulties. Check out George Zamfir's brilliant SlideShare 'Responsive Web Design & Accessibility' for more details.[32]

While responsive design is a no brainer these days, *adaptive design* – stripping away the non-core goals of a website to leave a simpler version that focuses on the core goals users wish to complete when they're on the move – isn't so universally accepted, even though it is at the heart of designing mobile apps. This is a shame as there is ample evidence that many disabled people prefer the simplicity of adaptive mobile sites over desktop ones, as this quote from The Atlantic's 'What the Shift to Mobile Means for Blind News Consumers' makes clear:[33]

'The shift to mobile – and the stripped down,
sparse aesthetic that in many cases comes
with it – makes web navigation easier for
someone using screen readers and other
tools designed to help people with varying
levels of sightedness. [Blind user Christopher
Danielson] will often log on to a website's
mobile iteration as a way to cut through the
clutter.'

If you do decide to include adaptive design on your
mobile website or app, the separation between core
and non-core goals that you made earlier in this
activity will guide you in deciding which goals to
leave out. And it is useful to include the ability for
users to choose to view the full or adaptive version
of a website on a mobile device in case they really do
want to apply for a mortgage on their smartphone –
see guidelines from the BBC.[34]

Mobile has forced product designers to be responsive
to the different capabilities of the *devices* people use
to view their products, so taking that further step
to be responsive to the different capabilities of the
people using them – as ISO 30071-1 requires – should
not be too much to ask. After all, if designers
changed their practices to design for the latest
advances in technology, such as retina screens, when

few people had devices that included them, why shouldn't they do the same for the needs of people with impairments who are far more numerous?

NOW IT'S YOUR TURN

Use the ICT system accessibility log template to guide you through considering what your approach to delivering accessibility on different devices and OSes should be.

ACTIVITY 3

Specify User Accessibility Needs

A ctivities 1 and 2 introduced you to the numbers and grouping of people with disabilities, the way they generally use digital products across devices, and the preferences and restrictions that arise from different contexts of use. Activity 3 takes that deeper to look at how those needs and preferences relate to your *specific* product's purpose, goals and tasks, and how to set the accessibility aims for your product.

You need to specify:

- The user accessibility needs of the product with reference to standards, or via integrating disabled users into your user research into the needs and preferences of audiences for your specific product

- Success criteria for the product's user goals, using the concept of accessibility experience

- The target browsers, OSes and assistive technologies your product will aim to provide this accessibility experience on

a. Integrating people with disabilities into your user research

Hopefully your user research (whether desk research or with real users) in activities 1 and 2 gave you valuable insights about how people generally use digital products. In this activity, we'll look into what free user research won't tell you: what your audiences with disabilities want from *your* product.

One way of specifying the user accessibility needs for your product is by reviewing lists of needs in accessibility standards like ISO/IEC 29138-1 and ISO/IEC Guide 71:2014 whose accessibility goals are summarised in Annex A of ISO 30071-1. ISO 30071-1 also suggests that you identify relevant accessibility guidelines for your *type* of product (such as WCAG 2.0 for desktop websites, WCAG 2.1 for mobile sites and apps, iOS accessibility guidelines[1] or Android accessibility guidelines[2] for native apps), and gives links to relevant sets of guidelines in its Annex C. These can be very helpful in identifying the user accessibility needs for your product, as well as providing guidelines to help meet those needs. You'll revisit the exact set of guidelines that you could use for your product in Activity 4.

In practice, what almost all organisations do is set the user accessibility needs for their product directly from guidelines like WCAG without another thought and move on. This is a handy shortcut, but it deprives them of any understanding of the needs and preferences of people with disabilities from their specific product. That's like deciding the only usability guidance you need for your project is a list of principles written in another country years ago. No organisation worth its salt does such a thing unless it cannot afford user research for its product, as they already realise the value of user research to tell them what they need to know for the design of their specific product in the current time and digital culture. ISO 30071-1 advocates that the same should apply for identifying user accessibility needs.

While accessibility guidelines like WCAG do a good job of identifying the user needs of many people with disabilities, they do have some gaps in representing the needs of *all* people with disabilities, so it is important to see how these needs may or may not cover all people with disabilities in the target audiences of your specific product. ISO 30071-1 suggests that where accessibility guidelines don't adequately cover key audiences for your product, for example, if you are creating a website specifically for autistic people, you could develop them yourselves.

ISO 30071-1 advises on how to go about achieving this: while ISO/IEC 29138-1 can give you a framework for creating guidelines yourself, a preferable way is for you to include disabled and older users in your user research into the needs and preferences of audiences for your product.

Your user research could be surveys, testing of competitor products or ethnographic research into the context, preferences and specific needs of the audiences for your product. This is the type of research that all leading organisations do before they start creating a product to make sure they know whether or not their 'great idea' is something that will attract an audience, whether it meets a need that actually exists, and how people might want to use the product if it does.

User research aims to provide reliable findings regarding:

- The context in which people may use your product

- The problem that they wish your product to solve for them

- Their preferences for how you should solve it

- How quickly and precisely your product needs to solve their problem, and whether or not there is a trade-off between those two things that they would accept

The aim is to more deeply understand the primary and secondary audiences you've already defined – the audience segmentation – to build up a picture of the different types of person in those audiences. To understand what makes one set of people different from another set of people, and how those differences impact the product you are creating. To understand whether one product could work for all of the different people who might want to use it, or whether you need to consider personalisation to satisfy all the people in your audiences.

To give you an analogy, Ford makes motor cars. Cars are designed to get you from A to B. So why does Ford have more than one model in its range of cars? And why for every model of car is there more than one engine size or specification of comfort and functionality extras?

This is all because of coarse and fine audience segmentation. There are many different types of person who might want to get from A to B. They may have different budget levels and passenger or baggage requirements. A single man's needs may be different from those of a mother with four kids. A young boy racer and an older person will have different feelings about speed. If I want my car to be a status symbol – if I want to 'pimp my ride' and make it look flash – my preferences will be different from someone who is not interested or cannot afford that. This is what spoilers were invented for.

Returning to your digital product, the question is: how many of the different segments of users can your one product satisfy? Does it make sense for it to be one product trying to serve everybody? Or does it make more sense, because the needs of everybody are different, to create product variants to meet those needs, the way the car industry has always done? To continue the car analogy, do your different audience segments want a different radio or engine, or do they want a different car?

We'll come back to these ideas of personalisation and product variants in Activity 5. At this point, it's important for us to do the user research to know how to make these decisions later in the process.

Communicating user needs across the product team

It's equally important to know how to communicate the findings of user research to people across your product team so they can best design a product that satisfies the needs of all your target audiences. Many design teams use *personas* to aid this communication, so it's important that your set of personas include the needs of people with disabilities – if 20% of the population has a disability, this representation needs to be reflected in your personas.

Here's Judith Fellowes, a UK freelance user researcher who is a leading expert in the field, talking on how best to do this in my interview with her:

'A persona is a representation of who your user might be. The idea behind it is that if you are designing for an individual, it works much better than just trying to design for everybody where you may end up with something that just doesn't work for anybody ... If you are focusing on an individual, then you can create something that's a lot more coherent.

'In reality, what you might be doing is... focusing on a couple of personas, a couple of people who have different needs. For example, you might be saying, "We've got this audience who are pretty technical and they can understand most things, and we've got this audience who perhaps need a helping hand."

'Access needs are part of so many people. At least 20% of the population have disabilities. Obviously, you're looking at how each persona relates to your product, because that's what you're working towards. But then you also need to understand how the access needs might impact on that. You know if somebody has got a disability or an access need, it doesn't necessarily take over their lives. It's not how they define themselves as individuals.

'So I think it's just being aware... If you've got a persona who is in their fifties, then statistically they might have a problem with their eyesight. They might be developing something like arthritis in their hands.

'Or people's impairments may explain their preferences. It's very possible that people represented by your "video junkie" persona may have a strong preference to use the video on your website because they are dyslexic.'

How user research can impact a site – a case study

Like many websites, version one of the Hassell Inclusion site had a lot of words on it. Which was fine for the relatively small number of people who are vision impaired, but not so good for the millions of people with literacy difficulties.

As my Accessibility Myths blogs and podcast[3] (a summary of some of my user-research findings that are most challenging to accepted ideas about accessibility) make clear, text is not the pinnacle of accessibility, despite most guidelines giving you that idea. At Hassell Inclusion, we know the 6.3 million people in the UK who are dyslexic and those with literacy and learning difficulties really appreciate being able to get the content of articles via non-text means. While making a video or audio equivalent of all of our blogs isn't practical, we specifically schedule video interviews and team podcasts to better suit the needs of people who don't like text, while also providing transcripts to ensure anyone who is hard of hearing can get things in the format they would like too.

Similarly, our desk research into device usage by the general population and our analysis of how people use our site on Google Analytics found that increasing numbers were viewing on mobile. While we would have done it anyway, this reinforced the requirement that version two of our site should be responsive to improve the experience of our users who browse on mobile.

NOW IT'S YOUR TURN

- Talk to your user-experience team to see if they are planning to do any user research to guide your product's creation, and request that people with disabilities are included in that research. Document the key findings in your ICT system accessibility log.

- Similarly, if they are planning to use personas, ask how the team plans to ensure the personas reflect the reality of disability within your product's target audiences.

b. Defining success criteria and setting the level of accessibility experience

This part of Activity 3 helps you to think about the success criteria for user goals in your product and the overall level of *accessibility experience* your product should aim to provide for its target audiences, depending on the purpose of the product. An online game that is usable but not fun isn't really a game. A page informing you of rubbish collection times needs to be easy to read but cannot really aim to be 'satisfying'. An online HR system that allows you to book leave, but does it slower than the call centre it replaced, is probably a bad investment. Aiming to deliver the wrong level will cost you – too high may make your development impossible; too low may make your development pointless.

Defining success criteria for the completion of each user goal

Now you've specified your core and non-core goals, it's important to specify success criteria for each user goal – how you'll define if your product is successful at enabling its target audiences to achieve the goal. What will success look like? This is important because it is what you will assess later on when you test the product during its creation in Activity 6.

In Activity 6, we'll look at ways of breaking down the user goal into all the steps that will be needed to take users on the user journey from start to end. Here, we need to consider two aspects of success for a user goal:

- *How many* of the goal's steps will users need to complete for it to have been a successful experience? Is the goal one where, if you can't complete all of the steps, it's not worth bothering at all? An example of this would be the 'find and buy' workflow of an online store. If you can't actually complete the purchase of a product you've found in the store, what value is there in being able to find it? Alternatively, for some goals there may be value in getting half of the way. Is the goal all or nothing, or can it be 'kind of OK'? This is what ISO Standard 9241-11 for the Human-Centred Design of Interactive Systems calls *'effectiveness'*.[4]

- Does the *efficiency* of completing the goal matter? If checkout is possible but slow (it's inefficient) then you may lose customers to more efficient rival retail sites over time.

How close do you need to be to full success to launch the product? You'll need to define this for each goal and for the product as a whole. And for accessibility, this definition is aided by the concept of *accessibility experience.*

Defining the level of accessibility experience

Right back to the original days of WCAG 1.0, with its Priority 1, 2 and 3 levels, accessibility guidelines have always included the idea of the different lengths you might choose to go to, to make a product accessible.

There's a lot about that idea that makes sense. After all, we all have different aims, different values that we use to decide how far we're going to go to make something happen. It's helpful to decide what your aims are, even if you can't always live up to them.

However, WCAG 2.0's A, AA and AAA levels, which replaced the numeric priority levels in WCAG 1.0, are crude ways of setting your accessibility aims. WCAG doesn't help you look at the cost benefits of choosing which of its different levels of accessibility would suit your digital product's accessibility ambition. It doesn't specify the *costs* of success criteria at different levels – the amount of work you'd have to do to live up to level A for alt-text for images is much smaller than the amount of work you'd have to do to meet level A for captions. And while the qualitative *benefits* to users described in each success criteria are useful, there are no quantitative figures of how many users would benefit, which would enable you to measure or compare the relative benefit of different levels.

Even more importantly, while WCAG strives to ensure all of its success criteria are testable, its levels of accessibility speak to the work you need to put in to make something accessible, not to the impact you wish that work to have on your target audiences. Remember, it's not what you do that matters; it's the effect it has.

To help product managers concentrate on what is important rather than lots of success criteria detail, ISO 30071-1 places the focus of your product's accessibility aims on the user of the product instead of the technical details of the product's implementation. It looks specifically at what quality of user experience your product will aim to provide for its users who have disabilities, which it calls the *level of accessibility experience*. This gives people with disabilities a relatable quality of user experience they can expect from a product rather than having to become experts in understanding what quality they will get from products that claim to be WCAG A, AA, or AAA compliant.

It's a myth that disabled people want 'accessible products'.[5] They want products that work for them, and they'll work out pretty quickly whether they do. If a product helps them achieve the thing that they came to it to do, then it's a good product. If it doesn't, it's not a good product, no matter what label you've stuck on it. So ISO 30071-1 distinguishes between three levels of accessibility experience that you might wish to provide for users with disabilities.

The lowest level is the *technical level*. This is where you follow technical accessibility guidelines to create your product, and where, theoretically, if all users use the right assistive technology and accessibility settings, they will be able to access it. That's the way most product owners use WCAG at the moment, but it doesn't mean your disabled and older users will actually be able to use your product.

The next level up is the *effective and efficient level*. This is essential; it is the level that is referenced, for example, in the UK's Equality Act, which requires you to take reasonable steps to make sure that disabled people can use your website or app. Not *access* it, but *use* it.

Digital products need to be usable. If they achieve the technical level but are not usable for a disabled person, then you are still potentially at risk under legislation like the Equality Act, and disabled people are also likely not to become your customers or recommend your product to anyone else. We all want to be able to use a digital product to effectively and efficiently complete the tasks we went to it to achieve. Anything less is not a good digital product, and users will only use it if they have no alternative – ie there is no other way they can get your services (for example, using a call centre or branch for information, rather than your site or app) and you have no competitors providing similar, more usable services.

The top level is the *satisfying level*. The ISO definition of usability[6] has always included three elements: efficiency, effectiveness and satisfaction. Efficiency and effectiveness are well placed in the middle level of accessibility experience, but satisfaction is difficult to pin down. It's the one element that ISO 30071-1 considers is better abstracted out to this level, as not all digital products are designed to be satisfying.

To give an example, how satisfying can it be for you to find your bank balance on your online banking service? That makes little sense. What you want is a banking site that is effective (where you can find your balance) and efficient (where you can find it quickly). I have no idea what satisfaction would feel like for this goal – unless the amount was higher than you expected.

Sometimes, though, 'satisfying', even 'enjoyable', can be central to the whole purpose of the product. If a game is not enjoyable, it's not a game. And the number of online games being created is constantly growing, especially with the current trend towards 'gamification' to drive user engagement with sites or apps that support tasks that are important but relatively mundane, like ensuring new bank staff learn regulatory requirements via e-learning.[7] If a game needs to be fun, it needs to achieve the 'satisfying' level of accessibility experience to have any point.

To give an example, let's take a game that's old enough for pretty much everyone to know: Pacman. You guide your Pacman around a maze, eating pills to score points while being chased by ghosts. When you've eaten all the pills in the maze, you get bonus points and advance to the next level.

The purpose of the game is fun, and fun comes from pitching the challenge of playing the game at the right level. You need to be able to win, but not so easily for there to have been no challenge at all. If the ghosts are too fast and there's no way of outrunning them, the game is frustrating. If the ghosts are too slow and it's easy to outrun them, the game is boring. Neither of those is fun.

Let's look at our levels of accessibility experience for playing online Pacman.

I'm going to do this from the perspective of someone who has limited ability with their hands. They may not be able to use a mouse or trackpad to control the computer. Let's say their ability to control the computer is restricted to one button, called a switch. When they want something to happen, they press the switch. They could be someone like Professor Stephen Hawking or a child with motor impairments and learning difficulties. Either way, they want to play online Pacman through their usual means of controlling the computer.

In this case, the 'technical' level must ensure the user can control Pacman using their switch. How could they use one switch to control Pacman, who normally needs up-down-left-right keys? Well, you could put a focus box on the screen that cycles continually between all of the directions: up, right, down, left, up, right, down, left. And when the focus reaches the direction that the user wants Pacman to go, they hit the switch and Pacman moves in that direction until they choose another direction. That makes it possible for one switch to enable Pacman to go in four different directions, so the user can play the game as long as they can wait long enough for the direction they want to go in to arrive in the cycling.

An 'effective and efficient' level of accessibility experience in this case means that the user must have a chance of winning. If the ghosts are quicker than the speed of cycling of their switch selector, then they cannot win, because while they're waiting for the focus to cycle, a ghost could come and eat their Pacman. To make the game usable, the speed of the ghosts' movement needs to adapt to the user's speed of interaction with the direction controls.

For the game to be 'satisfying', it needs the right level of challenge – not too easy, not too hard – and the user needs to be able to see progress in their score over time, against themselves and other people, as they get better at playing the game. They may also want to experience all the other things that make a game enjoyable. It's important, for example, the way something looks or sounds – that's why we have visual and audio designers to bring the right aesthetics and production values to the game. These things are all part of the experience.

While few digital products are games, I chose this example because the trends in digital user experience are to add satisfaction to as many digital products as possible, to make them more compelling to use. This is what the interest in gamification is all about. Applying game dynamics to dull products to make them more enjoyable can pay huge dividends for everything from e-learning to retail.

And these game dynamics are exactly those in the Pacman example – the fun, the challenge, the production values, the ability to play against friends in a league. So if more products are aiming to be enjoyable, you need them to provide a satisfying user experience to each user, including those with disabilities, because gamified products that only provide an 'effective and efficient' level of accessibility experience miss the whole point of the gamification.

Here, as usual, ISO 30071-1 doesn't dictate the level of accessibility experience to pick for your product. It lets you know what the options are and asks you to justify your choice of level, especially if you choose to just aim to provide the technical level.

The final point here is that pragmatically, you may need to aim for different levels of accessibility experience for the different combinations of user goal and user group that you have. Our example detailed how you could create online Pacman to give people using a switch a satisfying user experience. But maybe a person who is blind won't be able to play the game at all without you radically changing it. While I have created games that can be played purely using 3D audio and the keyboard or gesture,[8] that's too much of a challenge for most online games to reasonably accommodate.

You may need to say for that combination of user group and user goal (ie people who are blind who want to play the game) you will not attempt this, but it could be that there are other goals in the product – being in a high score table with your friends, for example – that you can make more accessible to more user groups.

It's important for you to set the accessibility aims for your product with your eyes open to user needs, and to what it may or may not be possible to support. You'll refine your understanding of how much work you'll need to do to achieve the level of accessibility experience you've chosen as you continue through the activities. And you may need to revisit and amend your aims if it becomes clear that you cannot achieve all of them.

This is where the segmentation of user goals into core and non-core that you explored in Activity 2 will help you. Some core goals may need to be 'satisfying' to support your product's purpose, but 'technical' might be enough for other goals because they are of lower priority for your users.

As digital products evolve to support more varied purposes, there could be even more interesting examples in the future. The challenges of accessibility should not constrain this innovation in product purposes, but people with disabilities should not be locked out from enjoying new directions when it is possible to meet their needs. And as Chapter 2 highlighted, some of the best innovations come from the challenge of meeting the needs of people with disabilities.

NOW IT'S YOUR TURN

- Use the ICT system accessibility log template to guide you through specifying a default level of accessibility experience that you will aim for in your product for all user groups and user goals. You could base this on a default level of accessibility experience that your organisation has set for all your digital products in your organisational ICT accessibility policy (see this book's companion, *Inclusive Design for*

Organisations, for more details), justifying any divergence from that if you consider it necessary for your product.

- Once you've decided this and documented it in the log, check all user goals and user groups to see if you need to downgrade the default level of accessibility experience for any of them. If you feel this is necessary, document it in the log along with your justification.

c. Defining your target browsers and assistive technologies

If you've chosen to aim for an accessibility experience beyond the technical level, you'll need to ensure that your product is usable in practice by people with disabilities in your target audiences. You've chosen not to hide behind guidelines for a legal view of accessibility, but to follow 'it's not what you do that matters, but the impact you have', so you need to engage with the realities of delivering accessibility through the browsers and assistive technologies people are likely to be using.

The choice of devices to support covered in Activity 2 was about balancing the benefits of maximising your audience by enabling them to get a good experience

of your products on all the devices that they have
with the costs of supporting each of those devices
and their OSes. The same balance is key for the
choice of the browsers and assistive technologies that
you will support on those devices.

How browser and assistive technology support impacts development and testing of websites

There's nothing new, or specific to accessibility,
about browser support. It has been a necessary
inconvenience for all web projects since the late
1990s. I remember writing my first browser-support
standard for the BBC[9] in 2001, and updating that
standard every quarter against analytics of the
browsers that our audiences used to view our site.

Browser support is a reflection of the reality that web
development is not as straightforward as the creators
of web standards and digital products would wish.
As web technologies such as HTML 5, CSS 3 and
WAI-ARIA are interpreted and presented to users
by browsers, it's important for the technology and
browser creators to agree on standard ways for how
this is done.

Ideally, all browser creators would follow web
standards in the same way, enabling website creators

to create one website which would work and look equally good on all browsers with no extra effort. Unfortunately, this has rarely if ever been the case, and the quirks of different browsers and different versions of browsers are always things that coders have had to test for and work around.

In this context, support for assistive technologies presents a new level of complication to those creating websites. Ideally, all assistive technology creators would follow the User Agent Accessibility Guidelines (UAAG)[10] in the same way. But unfortunately, as for browsers, this is not the case.

Different assistive technologies and different *versions* of the same assistive technology often provide a different user experience of the same website (see Steve Green's interview at the end of this activity). This is particularly true for additions to W3C specifications like the new native elements in HTML 5,[11] although most browsers and assistive technologies can now handle WAI-ARIA well.

There are a large and growing number of assistive technologies available for disabled people to use. On some OSes, a standard assistive technology for a particular disabled audience is available – for example, the VoiceOver screen reader comes as standard on all Apple devices. But for most OSes that don't have a standard assistive technology built in for each disabled audience, there are at least two competing options available to buy. And unfortunately for digital product owners, each often distinguishes itself from its competition by doing proprietary things that its competitors don't.

While there are more assistive technologies available than just screen readers, they are normally the cause of most development challenges as there are major variations in the way different screen readers create an interactive experience for vision-impaired users from the way that web pages are coded. This means that different screen readers may give a different user experience for the same website, unless you code around the quirks of each screen reader or version of a screen reader.

Worse than this, as assistive technologies interact with the browser to provide the user experience of a website, the same version of an assistive technology can sometimes give a different user experience of a site on different browsers. The result is that, for inclusive web development, assistive technology support is a multiplying factor on top of a project's browser-support policy. As any web test manager will tell you, the cost of testing is directly tied to the number of browsers you need to test a product against. And as any developer will tell you, it may take a lot of time to create code workarounds for browser (or assistive technology) quirks that testing identifies. Therefore, the addition of each browser and assistive technology to support can be a major factor in the costs for the project.

The fewer assistive technologies your product needs to support, the cheaper its development will be. So the question is how to decide which assistive technologies to support.

How to choose which browsers and assistive technologies to support

It's likely that the browsers your website will support will have already been defined via a standard browser-support policy for all your digital products. This may have been varied if the product is for a market where that is necessary – for example, supporting the UC browser for websites designed for countries where it has a big market share.[12] If you don't already have a browser-support policy, you could create one by looking at what the bigger sites are using – see the BBC's browser-support standards[13] or just google 'browser support'. If all else fails, deciding to support the latest version of all major browsers, and using tools like Modernizr[14] to make this easier, is usually a good start.

So we're really talking about assistive technology support as the choice you'll make in this activity. The first thing to take into account when making this decision is whether or not you have any ability to *control* the assistive technologies your target audiences will use. In the case of an intranet, you may be in control; unless you allow staff to 'bring their own device', you will provide all of the technology they use to interact with your intranet, including the assistive technologies that your disabled staff use.

To give an example, while there are at least five different screen readers available on the Windows platform, most organisations that provide screen readers for their staff standardise on one and make sure they have a policy in place for keeping all of their screen reader users up to date with the latest version. While this may cost in licence upgrades, the cost is far outweighed by the savings available from being able to specify that all intranet content and applications need to support just that one screen reader.

Unfortunately, the converse is true for publicly available websites. If you recall the example from Chapter 2, a blind pensioner was 'disgusted' that I had tested the BBC iPlayer with the most popular desktop screen reader in the UK – JAWS[15] – as the cost of a licence was three times the cost of his laptop and he could not afford it. The screen reader he chose to use was the free NVDA[16] which at the time could not handle the technologies used in iPlayer. This complaint kicked off what I believe was the first comprehensive screen reader usage survey, certainly in the UK, if not in the world. While the 'Screen Reader Testing Guidelines'[17] that resulted from it are now out of date, the results of similar annual WebAIM screen reader surveys[18] in the United States are an essential free online resource to help you make justifiable decisions about which screen readers to support. Beyond screen readers, gov.uk have also published useful insights from their wider 'Assistive Technology Survey 2016'.[19]

These surveys, and advice on the most popular *combinations* of assistive technology and browser that people use,[20] can help you choose a default set of assistive technologies to support for all your digital products. But different products from your organisation may have different purposes, audiences and production constraints. This means that, as in all ISO 30071-1's activities, it is up to the product manager and their product team to choose which assistive technologies to support for the particular product that they are creating, and to justify those choices.

The choice of the browsers and assistive technologies you will support will have a large impact on the planning and budget for accessibility testing that you'll find in Activity 6. So you may need to revisit Activity 3 if your test budget can't accommodate the costs of the support you've specified here.

NOW IT'S YOUR TURN

- Use the ICT system accessibility log template to guide you through considering what browsers and assistive technologies to support.

- If your product is a website, decide which browsers you will support across the different OSes of the devices you have chosen to support. Then decide which pairs of assistive technology and browser you will support, using the advice above and that of any accessibility testing organisations you choose to work with.

For insights into doing this, here's my interview with Steve Green from Test Partners, a digital product testing company in the UK:

'Within accessibility testing, we have got several services. WCAG testing is one, expert review with assistive technologies is another.

'WCAG testing is fairly straightforward because they are prescriptive, technical checkpoints. For a lot of the checkpoints in WCAG, it doesn't matter what browser you are testing because you are just looking at the code. For example, if it's semantically structured, that's always the same.

'There are only a few checkpoints where we test with different browsers, because we know from experience that we are going to get different results. One example is zoom. We know that some websites when you zoom them in Firefox behave differently than if you zoom them in Internet Explorer. So part of our standard approach is to test that checkpoint with two or more browsers. Depending on the content, that might apply to some other checkpoints – dynamic content, hide/reveal and tabbed interfaces might also behave differently in different browsers.

'In our expert review, we will typically test with screen readers, screen magnifiers and voice recognition software. Within screen readers, obviously you have got JAWS, NVDA, Window-Eyes and VoiceOver, and all of those will behave differently from each other. On top of that, each version of those will behave differently from the other versions, and it can even depend on what OS they are sitting on.

'There is a colossal number of permutations, so we have to take a pragmatic approach to which ones to test, depending on the client's budget.

We might have to pick perhaps the most recent JAWS version and the version two or three back, the latest NVDA, the latest VoiceOver, and maybe an older version of each of those.

'Invariably we find we get significantly different results on each of them.

'Sometimes this is because of a non-compliance in the code – it's not written to standards – in which case the first thing to do is to correct that. Sometimes it is down to ambiguities in the standards and specifications. Sometimes it's down to a bug in the assistive technology or the browser.

'Then you have got to consider: is it possible and worthwhile to do a work around? Once we see what the results are, we can have a discussion with the client with regards to the impact. Because although two screen readers might behave differently, they might still give an acceptable user experience. It's only if there is an actual negative impact on users that we need to start thinking about remediation.

'I'm all about the user experience. I am not concerned *why* something doesn't work for people; what I'm concerned about is *that* it doesn't work. For me, there are only two important people on a development project: the product owner and the end user. I am coming from their perspective: that we should do whatever's necessary to give a good user experience.

'Coding to standards is where you start, but it's not enough. People still expect to do browser compatibility and fix anything that doesn't look or behave right, so I find it disappointing if they aren't prepared to do the same thing for assistive technologies. I can't think of any rationale for not doing it.

'Clients always ask what it's going to cost. That depends on how much they want to understand what they've built. The more budget they give us, the more assistive technologies and browsers we can test with, and the more they will know.

'Testing is about risk management. If you have no knowledge, you can't manage your risk. The more you know, the more you can do about it. You can either fix things, or mitigate anything that doesn't work by some other means. Even if you don't do anything about it, at least you've quantified the risk: the percentage of users you are going to lose. If you don't test, you don't know.'

ACTIVITY 4

Specify Accessibility Requirements

N ow you're almost ready to design and develop your product. You need to plan tactically to ensure accessibility is well covered across each part of your process and monitor your team's work so the product you deliver meets your intended accessibility aims.

In design and development, you make the largest number of decisions which impact your product's accessibility. These are detailed decisions rather than the strategic ones in the previous activities. To be able to make these decisions well, you need to specify the *functional accessibility requirements* that designers, developers and content authors need to deliver to address the needs of your product's users. These will also be essential if you are not going to create the product in-house, but plan to outsource its development or procure it as a commercial off-the-shelf (COTS) solution.

Adopting WCAG as your functional accessibility requirements is the established way of doing this. However, while this is convenient, the set of accessibility guidelines you reference should be impacted by the *implementation technologies* you'll use to create your product. You'll also find that you may want to adopt most of the guidelines as requirements, but not to use all of them because they don't suit your product's aims. You may also need to add other requirements that aren't referenced in the guidelines.

If you're going to use *enabling technologies* like CMSs or JavaScript frameworks to help you build the product, you'll also need to carefully consider their accessibility capabilities before selecting them, so authoring tool guidelines like ATAG could also form part of your requirements.

Activity 4 is all about:

- Specifying the implementation and enabling technologies that you'll use to create the product

- Finding appropriate technical accessibility guidelines for those technologies to help speed up the specification of the product's accessibility requirements

- Using those requirements to ensure accessibility if you contract out or procure the product

a. Specify your product's implementation technologies

Whether you are creating the digital product yourself, procuring it or outsourcing it to other organisations to build, the *implementation technologies* used in its creation are a key element that impacts on how accessible you can make it. Activity 4 starts with defining the implementation technologies to be used in the product's creation, which were introduced in the accessibility ecosystem in Activity 2.

If you're creating the product bespoke, then the choice of implementation technologies is up to you. If you're outsourcing it, you'll need your supplier to choose the technologies as wisely as you would. So how do you ensure the implementation technologies chosen will allow you to create a product that is accessible?

For websites, the rich capabilities of HTML 5, CSS 3 and JavaScript have all but made previously essential non-W3C implementation technologies like Flash and Silverlight unnecessary. If you do need to go beyond HTML, CSS and JavaScript, then check any technology that you consider using provides *WCAG techniques documentation*,[1] like W3C's technologies do. If it does, then following those techniques will enable your coders to use best practice for making accessible products with the technology in alignment with WCAG.

If WCAG techniques do not exist for the technology, then you'll need to examine it further to check whether it exposes content, structure and functionality to assistive technologies and allows products created in it to live up to WCAG's POUR principles.

WCAG'S POUR PRINCIPLES

WCAG success criteria are organised around four principles which lay the foundation necessary for anyone to access and use web content. Anyone who wants to use the web must have content that is:

- Perceivable – information and UI components must be presentable to users in ways they can perceive (they can't be invisible to all of the user's senses).

- Operable – UI components and navigation must be operable. The interface cannot require interaction that a user cannot perform.

- Understandable – users must be able to understand information and the operation of the UI.

- Robust – content must be robust enough to be interpreted reliably by a wide variety of user agents, including assistive technologies. Users must be able to access the content as technologies advance.

If any of these criteria is not met, users with disabilities will not be able to use the web. While these principles were created for the web, they also apply for apps.

The key technology challenge these days comes from apps for mobile and many other device categories which are coded in different languages and using different APIs, depending on the OS of the device. For example, while hybrid apps for iOS and Android can be created in HTML, CSS and JavaScript with a Cordova[2] wrapper, native apps for iOS are coded in Swift and native apps for Android are coded in Java.

Apps also bypass the browser accessibility settings layer in the accessibility ecosystem which has provided accessibility customisation for years. So app developers need to look more closely at how the APIs they use for creating mobile apps will interface with accessibility settings in the device's OS and assistive technologies that are part of the OS, and those that can be installed onto the device (something Android facilitates more than iOS).

As different OSes provide different levels of accessibility support, it is entirely possible that – unless you provide 'additional accessibility measures' in the app itself (as we'll discuss in Activity 5) – the accessibility you will be able to deliver in the versions of your app for various OSes will be different. Take this into account when you're reviewing the choices that you made in Activity 2 for which mobile OSes to support and whether your apps will be native or hybrid.

b. Specify your product's enabling technologies

While implementation technologies are more supportive of accessibility than ever before, few websites or apps are built from scratch these days. Most websites are now built:

- On top of an underlying CMS such as Drupal or WordPress

- Using a JavaScript framework and library of prebuilt components to quickly add modern site functionality, such as React JS or Angular JS

- Including embedded widgets such as media players from YouTube, Vimeo[3] or Brightcove;[4] global comment systems like Disqus;[5] or the ubiquitous social media buttons provided by Facebook, Twitter and LinkedIn

These enabling technologies are empowering website owners to create their own sites without needing to learn how to master implementation technologies or contract someone else to do it for them. However, different CMSs, frameworks and widgets may have different levels of support for accessibility built in. So how do you ensure that the technology shortcut you are about to select will allow you to create an accessible product?

Look out for any mention of accessibility and conformance with WCAG or ATAG.[6] ATAG is a set of guidelines that authoring tool (CMS) creators can follow to ensure their tools are able to produce accessible digital products (see also the discussion in Activity 8 on how CMSs which conform with ATAG can help uphold accessibility during post-launch site content maintenance). If accessibility isn't mentioned in the technology's documentation, ask its owner directly what level of accessibility support it provides and if accessibility improvements are scheduled in its development roadmap.

To give an example, the standard installation of WordPress – the most popular 'website builder' out there, and the one used to build the Hassell Inclusion website[7] – does allow you to create accessible websites. However, most WordPress themes – the mechanism you use for setting how your website will look and what functionality it will contain over and above the default WordPress functionality – have not been built with accessibility in mind. Similarly, most WordPress plugins – the mechanism WordPress uses for further extending site functionality into providing newsletters and aiding SEO, for example – have also not been built with accessibility in mind. This means that while WordPress can be used to create accessible websites, most professionally produced WordPress themes and plugins that allow you to quickly build an impressive, professional, capable website are currently unavailable to organisations that also wish to ensure their website is accessible.

This is what Graham Armfield of my Hassell Inclusion team, who is also a member of the 'Make

WordPress Accessible' team and makes WordPress sites for clients, had to say when I interviewed him:

'There's nothing in WordPress itself to hinder the accessibility of a website – I'm constantly working to make sure that's the case. But when you start off with a WordPress website, you need a theme of some sort. So your site's accessibility depends on whether or not the person who built that theme actually thought about accessibility.

'There are thousands of themes out there that are free to use. Unfortunately, few of those are accessible. The plugins would also need accessibility baked in. And it's not a panacea – there's still a responsibility on the content authors to follow simple accessibility guidelines when they're creating content.

'Some of my clients have been referred by people who have valued the accessibility that I've put into their sites. Others have come to me having never heard of accessibility. So during the requirements process when we're talking about the website that they would like, I always mention it. Many people have never thought about how people who are blind or motor impaired, for example, would use their website. But when you explain it to them, they really get it.'

For an up-to-date understanding of the accessibility of popular CMSs and JavaScript frameworks, please see my popular blog: 'What's new in Accessibility in 2019 – standards, authoring tools, frameworks and design thinking'.[8]

Why create a website at all when you can use a social media platform?

An even more pressing issue, which may finally be getting some attention in the communications and accessibility communities,[9] is how accessibility is impacted by the trend for organisations to dispense with a website completely and create a product page on a third-party platform like Facebook instead. By making this decision, they are making themselves dependent on the accessibility features that Facebook provides.[10]

Almost all organisations now use Facebook, Twitter, YouTube, Instagram, SoundCloud, SlideShare and other social media websites to extend their site's rich-media content capabilities and act as further channels to communicate with their audiences. While it makes commercial sense to use many channels to communicate with your audiences, this multi-channel approach to audience engagement presents challenges for accessibility. You must take into account the accessibility of your presence on *each* of these channels, most of which is not under your control. So your content strategy needs to include a pragmatic constraint that all important messages communicated on social media must also be communicated on the *most accessible* of your channels, which in many cases will be your website, over whose underlying technology and design you have most control.

Accessibility presence in two camps

The number of available implementation and enabling technologies is likely to continue growing in the future. So the community working on accessibility needs to be present in each of two camps:

- Those who are working to create implementation and enabling technologies that have accessibility baked in

- Those who are working to select the most suitable of these technologies from which to create accessible digital products

The first camp needs to contain experts in creating technologies that have accessibility baked in from the start, aligning with guidelines like ATAG and WCAG, and communicating the accessibility properties of their technologies in a language that product owners can understand. This will allow the second camp to more easily search for technologies that support all of their requirements, including accessibility. This may often require difficult decisions to be made where the most suitable components to meet the product owner's wider set of requirements do not meet their accessibility requirements. These are some of the biggest challenges for accessibility in the future.

For the creators of authoring tools, themes and plugins to take accessibility seriously as a requirement for their work, they need to feel the demand for accessibility from product owners. ISO 30071-1 helps raise the bar here by ensuring that product owners are clear about what their accessibility requirements are and why accessibility is important to them, so technology creators will have more motivation to bake in accessibility.

c. Using technical accessibility guidelines to specify accessibility requirements

When you're designing and developing the product, the number of decisions made per day goes through the roof. Now you're into technical rather than strategic decisions, and they need to be made more frequently and quickly. They're also being made iteratively – you're likely to go around the process of making a decision, checking its results and revisiting the decision to tweak it. And the number of people who make decisions also expands hugely, as does the number of locations in which they are making those decisions.

Responsibility for decision making needs to be devolved from the core team led by the product manager to staff who could be working all over the globe and various suppliers who may be developing different parts of the product. And all of these may be making decisions in break-out sessions, email discussions, daily stand-ups or on their own.

Functional and non-functional accessibility requirements

These people are unlikely to have the specialist expertise or time to research which of the many technical decisions they make every day will impact the accessibility of the product. But they still need to know how to make the decisions that do in a way that includes as many users as reasonably possible, so on top of the strategic research and decisions from the previous activities – all gathered in the ICT system accessibility log for easy reference – your team needs a clear set of *accessibility requirements* to follow in design and development.

Accessibility requirements split into:

- **Non-functional requirements.** These are the strategic decisions made in other accessibility activities, such as what devices, browsers and assistive technologies the product will support and whether it will use a single-design strategy or also include a user-personalised/ individualised strategy (see next activity).

- **Functional requirements.** These are detailed requirements that can be applied in the design, development and testing of the product to ensure it meets the user accessibility needs you found in

Activity 3. They are often specified in terms of the intended outcome of interacting with the system, the success criteria for achieving the outcome and any applicable conditions under which the requirement applies.

While the non-functional requirements are easy to capture, the functional requirements can take more time. There are two ways of doing this:

- Evaluate all the identified user accessibility needs from the previous activities to select which you'll transform into functional requirements

- Do what every other organisation does and use existing technical accessibility guidelines as the basis of these requirements, which speeds up their specification immensely

Using guidelines to create functional accessibility requirements

This just makes sense. Technical accessibility guidelines like WCAG have been created by accessibility experts, based on their understanding of the needs and preferences of people with impairments and how those needs impact those people when they use digital products. They explain how designing or coding pages in a particular way can give people a user experience which suits their needs and provide success criteria that can be used directly in testing.

The ideal technical accessibility guidelines are those that your team can rely on to be a complete guide: each guideline and success criterion needs to be necessary, and the whole set must be sufficient to satisfy all of the user needs of your target audiences to help you deliver a digital product that meets the level of accessibility experience you specified in Activity 3. Furthermore, these guidelines need to be appropriate for the type of product you are developing (see Activity 2), the audiences it is designed for and the devices it supports (see Activity 1), and the implementation and enabling technologies you will use to create it (this activity). Your team also need the guidelines to be a stable measure to audit your product against in testing, as we'll discuss in Activity 6.

However, as no set of guidelines could ever predict the future of what digital products could be or become, or replace well-researched local, product-specific expertise where it is available, you also need them to include a sensible exception process to handle new situations that their creators hadn't anticipated. Guidelines should never be the end of the discussion; they are its start. They're a gift, not a straitjacket.

Here's what Sarah Lewthwaite, Research Associate in Education at King's College, London, said when I interviewed her:

'One of my concerns with WCAG is that a standards perspective can be idealised and static. It gives you one view on a particular terrain, and in doing so it can obscure other perspectives. With WCAG you're trying to hit a checklist, so there may be alternative ways forward which are then difficult to see or pick up because you're focusing on this conformance/compliance issue. There isn't space within that checklist for other voices – maybe a developer's voice or a disabled user's voice, which of course is important. It doesn't leave room for that kind of personal usability testing, which is where we make knowledge about accessibility.

'Whereas, one of the strengths of BS 8878 (and ISO 30071-1) is the way it draws on more local expertise. The person using the standard can apply themselves and their knowledge, and engage the knowledge of those around them, to create maybe more robust, effective outcomes. It offers a framework that allows people making decisions to develop their expertise, rather than hit a checklist.'

To help team members make justifiable decisions, as part of an exception process, they need each success criterion to include the sort of *cost-benefits information* they need for all good decisions – in this case, which group of people the success criterion helps, by how much, and how many people there are in that group; and how much it is likely to cost to implement the techniques needed to follow the success criterion.

To help in deciding on exceptions prompted by lack of resource in the team, you need to know if any of the success criteria are *more important* than others and so should be prioritised (for example, because they bring greater benefits or are less costly to implement). Also, you need to know if there are *links and dependencies* between success criteria (for example, if one success criterion only solves a user's need if you've already followed another), so if you opt out of one, you might as well opt out of both as you won't get any value out of following the second success criterion. In many sets of guidelines, this information is provided through the concept of *levels* of conformance, or segmentation of guidelines into 'musts', 'shoulds' and 'coulds'.

Finally, your team needs a quick way of summarising any accessibility decisions they make in their ICT system accessibility log. The technical accessibility guidelines you choose should be *easy to reference* so your team can quickly state what set of guidelines they've conformed to and only note down any places where they have diverged from it – what success criteria they didn't follow and why they considered them to be justifiable exceptions.

Which technical accessibility guidelines to use to direct your product's creation

You need to decide which set of available technical accessibility guidelines are the best approximation to the ideal set, plan for how to use them most effectively during development and find ways of enriching them where they aren't ideal.

The default set of technical accessibility guidelines used by almost all organisations is WCAG, from the W3C, whose frequently used 2.0 version has been ratified as international standard ISO/IEC 40500:2012.[11] While WCAG 2.0 and the more recent version 2.1[12] aren't perfect, they are a massive achievement and gift to accessible web development as they encompass most of the success criteria that are important when you are developing a website on desktop (and mobile if you use 2.1). They also provide at least one implementation technique for achieving each success criterion, enabling:

- Interaction designers to understand how the needs of disabled people impact how they create information architectures and interaction design wireframes

- Visual designers to understand how the needs of disabled people impact how they create visual designs

- Client-side coders to understand how to create accessible semantic HTML and CSS that, when viewed through assistive technologies, meets the needs of disabled people

- Content creators to understand how the needs of disabled people impact their creation of text, images, audio and video

WCAG includes a large number of success criteria that people with each of these job roles can use to check their work for particular issues which impact the accessibility of the product. While the value of WCAG 2.0[13] and its achievability has been questioned,[14] much work has been done globally to establish it as the world's top harmonised technical accessibility standard – it's the most-known accessibility standard in most countries, and has been directly referenced in legislation such as the EU directive on accessibility of public websites and mobile apps,[15] Canada's Accessibility for Ontarians with Disabilities Act (AODA)[16] and the US Section 508 Refresh.[17]

As such, it's the obvious set of guidelines to *start* with.

But that's not the *end* of the story. WCAG 2.0 is not the *only* set of technical accessibility guidelines available, and – depending on the type of digital product you are creating – other guidelines can be useful in place of WCAG, or used together with WCAG to better guide accessibility work on *your* product.

Here's a guide to deciding which guidelines you will use to inform your product's development, depending on its product type, delivery platform and target audiences.

How the product's purpose influences your guideline choice

The most common example of a product type that benefits from the addition of another set of accessibility guidelines to WCAG 2.0 is rich internet applications. A great many digital products these days include complex or transactional interactions, whether they are online banking sites or online 'software as a service' replacements for desktop applications like word processors or webmail portals. While HTML 5 includes native components that have accessibility built in for these websites, where your developers create any custom components they may need to add WAI-ARIA[18] (often abbreviated to ARIA) to make them accessible.

If the digital product you are creating includes any authoring elements that allow users to create content in the product (eg a rich-text editor for adding comments), review the Authoring Tool Accessibility Guidelines (ATAG)[19] to advise you in including requirements to ensure that content created is accessible, as well as the authoring interface being accessible to people who have disabilities.

Finally, as online games are becoming more and more prevalent, and are a big challenge to make accessible, using specialised game accessibility guidelines[20] rather than WCAG may best help you cater for the needs of gamers with disabilities and other impairments.

How the product's implementation technology influences your guideline choice

If your product includes non-W3C implementation technologies, WCAG already covers some of these – like Adobe Flash, for example – through its techniques documents.[21]

However, some implementation technologies have their own separate guidelines. Digital products that need to include electronic documents, such as PDFs, for reasons of security or precision of formatting, should use PDF/UA[22] – the universal accessibility standard for PDFs, also known as ISO 14289-1 – to define what accessibility means for PDFs and to provide document authors with a clear means of achieving WCAG 2.0 conformance. EPUB is an alternative electronic document technology which is very accessible.[23]

As well as knowing the technical accessibility guidelines for creating electronic documents, efficiently embedding accessibility into your process for authoring them is key. Here's what Shannon Kelly, an Accessibility Subject Matter Expert for PDF documents, said when I interviewed her:

'We know PDF is not going to go away – many organisations are regulated to have a PDF format as their official record for archive. And customers often need documents like bank statements as proof they are financially capable, so banks provide them online as PDFs.

'Unfortunately, the software organisations use to create PDFs often doesn't include the tagging they need to be accessible. I set up teams of anywhere from 75 to 100 operators to manually tag documents for the Federal Government. It simply didn't scale. There are now a lot of automation tools that will allow tags to be applied to a PDF. But they aren't necessarily the right tags in the right order.

'So I created a solution where you get a human to build a template for the structured data – how a document should be read, in what order, and how the elements on a page should react with screen readers – and you apply the accessibility rules to that template. You create one template, then all the data that flows through that template can come out perfectly accessible – properly tagged, compliant to WCAG 2.0 Level AA – at the other end.'

Implementation technologies for mobile – websites and apps – are likely to have the greatest impact on your choice of technical accessibility guidelines. While the POUR principles at the heart of WCAG hold no matter what device you are creating products for, WCAG 2.0's success criteria are based on the presumption of a desktop computer with mouse and keyboard, and support from browser accessibility settings and assistive technologies.

For *mobile websites*, differences in mobile device capability (screen size, input devices, sensors and the like) and context of use require some of WCAG 2.0's success criteria to be *reinterpreted* to be appropriate. Thankfully, WCAG 2.1 has been created to step into this breach and includes new guidelines around on-screen touch and the orientation of the device. As few websites these days are designed solely for desktop, I'd recommend you read my 'WCAG 2.1 is here – what's in it for you?'[24] blog to see if WCAG 2.1 is a better set of technical accessibility guidelines for your website than WCAG 2.0.

For *mobile apps*, the accessibility guidelines of the OS you are developing for are equally, if not more, important than WCAG. Unfortunately, you will need to get on top of the different accessibility guidelines for each OS you are developing apps for, and then work out how they link back with WCAG 2.1 if you wish to harmonise your guidelines across the devices you support.

Thankfully, the BBC's Mobile Accessibility Guidelines[25] can help you through some of this complexity. They include a single set of sensible accessibility checkpoints for mobile websites and apps, with implementation techniques for HTML 5, iOS and Android for each checkpoint. While they don't link these checkpoints with WCAG success criteria, it is not particularly hard to do this, as we at Hassell Inclusion have done for our clients.

How the product's target audiences influence your guideline choice

The final thing to take into account when choosing accessibility guidelines is the impact of the user needs and preferences of the *target audiences* for your product, which we looked at in Activity 1.

This is important as there can be situations where the assumptions underlying WCAG do not hold for your audience. To give an example: WCAG's guidance for making websites accessible for blind people assumes they will be using screen readers to access websites, but this often doesn't hold for blind children. In my time as Accessibility Editor and Special Educational Needs Commissioner on *BBC Jam*, my challenge was to ensure that the e-learning games we were creating to help five- to sixteen-year-old children in the UK learn different curriculum subjects were accessible.

One essential bit of user research, which ensured that we didn't make the wrong strategic choices in our approach to accessibility, was the finding that no blind child below the age of eight in the UK was using a screen reader. If we had made our maths games accessible following WCAG and required five- to seven-year-old blind children to use screen readers to play them, most of the challenge in the games would have been in how to learn to use a screen reader. Learning maths skills, in comparison, is much easier.

Thankfully, our user research found this before we started any work, so we created Adobe Flash-based e-learning games which used simple keyboard skills, audio soundscapes and text to speech directly, rather than through a screen reader. We had to make our own functional accessibility requirements, not just follow WCAG.

Similar findings are apparent with the ageing population. WAI-AGE conducted research into the similarities and differences between the user needs of disabled people and older people, who increasingly experience multiple minor impairments as they age (see my interview with Andrew Arch below). It found many similarities in needs, and that WCAG is useful for making sure that older people can get a good user experience of websites.

It also found that older people are less confident in their use of accessibility settings in browsers, and in purchasing and installing assistive technologies, so they may benefit from websites that do not require them to have the right assistive technologies to get an accessible user experience.

If older people feature heavily in your target audiences, consider referencing guidelines that specialise in the needs of older people in your functional requirements – notably WAI-AGE's own 'Web Accessibility for Older Users: A Literature Review'[26] and the National Institute on Aging (NIA) and National Library of Medicine (NIH/NLM) resource 'Making your Website Senior Friendly'.[27]

This is what Andrew Arch, Leader of the WAI-AGE work on the link between accessibility, older people and mobile usage, said when I interviewed him:

> 'The older you get, the more likely you are to have vision problems as well as the normal degradation of sight with contrast acuity and those types of things that go with it. And your sight isn't the only thing that deteriorates as you get older – people's dexterity deteriorates, they need larger print...

> 'The European Commission is very interested in ageing, because in a number of European

countries, the proportion of people in the over-sixty-five age group is going up dramatically. It was looking at things like smartphones to keep in touch with the community, being able to do shopping online – all that sort of stuff helps somebody to maintain their independence for longer.

'We've got the baby boomers moving into retirement, expecting to continue to use computers. I've been told by people that they've actually got their magnifying glass out to read the computer screen because they didn't know how to make the fonts bigger. We know all this stuff about helping those we traditionally refer to as people with disabilities. How much of that applies to older people? Well, a lot of what the W3C and WCAG have documented applies directly.

'What we also found was that usability stuff like consistent navigation and consistent presentation, rather than the technical solutions, made a big difference to them. But most people aren't interested in learning how to use a screen reader when they turn eighty. They just want to use their computer the way the rest of the family uses it, not to have to use some weird bit of technology.'

To summarise, my advice is to consider WCAG and any specialist technical accessibility guidelines that are appropriate for your product purpose, audiences, devices and implementation technologies. You will find many overlaps and some contradictions. Where contradictions appear and the right one to overrule the others isn't clear, or you can't find any respected technical accessibility guidelines specific to the device, technology or product type you're creating, find an accessibility specialist to advise you on creating your functional accessibility requirements directly.

How to make decisions around conformance levels and exceptions

Once you've decided on the guidelines you'll use, the next issue you need to decide is how to approach the idea of conformance to the guidelines. And if the guidelines you are using include the idea of conformance levels, like WCAG does, what level of conformance should you decide to adopt?

WCAG defines three levels of conformance for success criteria: A (the lowest), AA, and AAA (the highest).[28] These originally approximated to the idea that level A success criteria were the musts, level AA were the shoulds and level AAA were the coulds, but over the course of time and people's experience of using WCAG 2.0, most accessibility experts and legislators have slightly moved the goalposts. These days the consensus agrees that achieving AA – satisfying all the level A *and* level AA success criteria – is essential for delivering a reasonable level of technical accessibility; and level AAA success criteria are coulds because the additional benefits of achieving them are not sufficiently proven.[29]

The obvious decision here might seem to be to choose the level of WCAG conformance which corresponds to the level of accessibility experience you chose in Activity 3. Unfortunately, the link between ISO 30071-1's three levels (technical, effective and efficient, and satisfying) and WCAG's three levels (A, AA and AAA) is not one-to-one. All three WCAG levels are really different sub-levels of ISO 30071-1's technical level of accessibility experience.

Many of WCAG's success criteria address usability issues, especially around the usability of forms, but WCAG 2.0 only includes 'those guidelines that address (usability) problems particular to people with disabilities' and not all the guidelines necessary 'to make content more usable by all people, including those with disabilities'.[30]

So, if you wish to deliver a user experience that is usable or satisfying for everyone, you will need to add other usability and user-experience guidelines to WCAG.

While WCAG 2.0 and 2.1 aren't everything you need, each set of guidelines does provide a good baseline to work from, and the conformance levels it defines quickly give you an understanding of each success criterion's relative importance. You can just pick a conformance level to aim for, which summarises all of the success criteria at that level and the levels below it.

This simplifies documentation of your accessibility decisions and allows you to easily 'badge' your level of conformance, which can be useful if you need to prove your accessibility level to regulators or legislators. These are two of the requirements of an ideal set of guidelines – and WCAG's authors have done much of the thinking for you...

Unfortunately, WCAG has two deficiencies against those requirements for an ideal set of guidelines, which complicate its value to projects:

1. **Limited cost-benefits consideration.** While WCAG does give some idea of the groups of disabled people who might benefit from each

success criterion, the assignment of levels to success criteria does not take into account the number of people in those groups (which is useful for assessing its cumulative benefit), nor the relative cost of implementing the techniques to achieve it.

For example: the number of people who benefit from captions being provided for video content is huge and the cost is reasonable, whereas the number of people who benefit from AD being added to video is small and the cost is large, yet both are set at the same level A in WCAG 2.0,[31] and none of this essential cost-benefits information is mentioned in the success criteria.

WCAG's choice to only include limited information on the benefits of a success criterion and no information on its costs in the documentation undercuts people's confidence in relying on a success criterion's conformance level to estimate the resource costs of using their implementation techniques or prioritise their accessibility work.

2. **Conformance as perfection.** The first deficiency is exacerbated by WCAG's definition of conformance as perfection in achieving all the success criteria at a given level.[32] Quite sensibly, the creators of WCAG didn't want to require

you to understand the links and dependencies between individual success criteria, so they made the success criteria at A, AA and AAA all internally consistent – the things that depend on each other, at every level, are included.

However, this emphasis on needing to achieve all of the success criteria on each level completely misunderstands the realities of digital product development – in website development, perfection is not something you strive for; you aim for continuous, pragmatic improvement over versions. And, unfortunately, if you need to break this consistency and opt out of a particular success criterion – for example, opting out of the need to include AD on all of the video on your VOD site – WCAG 2.0's 'statement of partial conformance'[33] exception process is weak and unsupportive. It is only defined for third-party content, is rarely understood or respected by organisations that use WCAG 2.0 AA as a legislative battering ram, and does not provide you with enough advice to make these exception decisions through justifiable reasoning.

When you are considering opting out of a success criterion, you need to know what the implications of that are – an estimate of the number of people who might have benefited and now won't, and whether opting out will deprive some of the other guidelines that you do follow of the effect they are supposed to have. WCAG's process gives you neither.

Organisations' frustration with the combination of WCAG's two deficiencies has prompted some to complain that accessibility is a 'ruinous obligation' as they don't feel free to make exceptions when they clearly need them.[34] A more useful reaction has been the creation of additional exception processes, like Holland's 'comply or explain' principle,[35] that sit on top of WCAG 2.0.

I don't believe that it is unreasonable to require organisations to conform with WCAG 2.0 or 2.1 in general. It makes sense for organisations to educate their staff in how to apply the guidelines to their work (as recommended in the 'Embedding competence and confidence' section in Chapter 4 of this book's companion, *Inclusive Design for Organisations*) and require them to do that, even if WCAG is not perfect. You don't throw the baby out with the bathwater.

I do believe, though, that it is unreasonable when staff have taken time to understand a particular success criterion (its benefits to users, the implications to those users of not following it and its implementation techniques) to require them to conform to it when the implementation techniques are too difficult or costly to follow in practice on their product. People have a 'gut' for this. They know when something feels wrong. They know it's wrong to be forced to abandon creating some useful functionality for a product because they can't make it accessible. They know that if they are spending 80% of their time on a feature implementing its accessibility, rather than balancing that time with other quality measures like performance or security, that is unreasonable. The tail should not wag the dog.

My advice on how to work around WCAG's deficiencies in a robust and justifiable way is:

- Use the WCAG 2.0 or 2.1 variants of the Accessibility Issue Prioritisation Matrix (included in the support materials of this book) to give you estimates for:

  - The cost benefits of each WCAG success criterion (calculated from the estimated cost of implementing its techniques, the estimated benefit based on the number of people affected and the severity of the impact of the success criterion on their ability to use a product)

  - Information on any dependencies or links between success criteria to inform your exception decision making

- Don't get hung up on WCAG conformance levels. Pick AA – it's the level that most people agree on, so it's the most sensible baseline. And for risk-mitigation reasons, it is the most commonly accepted 'safe answer' for WCAG conformance, so should keep you out of trouble if people insist on using WCAG's levels as a blunt instrument against you. Then add success criteria from other sets of guidelines that are needed for your product into your functional accessibility requirements.

- Give yourself permission to subtract guidelines during your development where the exception is *justifiable*. Document this baseline and exceptions.

- Spend less time defending your sensible, pragmatic exception decisions and more time concentrating on the more important issue, which is: can all your target audiences actually use your product?

If you use WCAG in this way, you'll get the benefit of all the great thought that went into WCAG 2.0 and 2.1 while being allowed to think for yourself – informed by the Accessibility Issue Prioritisation Matrix, your own local experience, and the research and decisions you've made earlier in ISO 30071-1's activities – when your product's needs are at variance with a success criterion.

If you haven't downloaded the book's support materials yet, I'd recommend you do so now – details are in the 'Support materials to accompany this book' section in the Introduction.

If you need more support for justifying this sensible course of action, see my popular blog 'The future of WCAG – maximising its strengths not its weaknesses'[36] for a fuller discussion. And be encouraged by what Sarah Lewthwaite, Research Associate in Education at King's College London, said when I interviewed her:

> 'Being able to handle ambiguity is an essential part of being an accessibility expert. One of the constrictions of WCAG is also its strength in the sense that it gives people a very black and white view of what's achievable: what hits the mark, what doesn't hit the mark… And that's why I think it is being picked up internationally: it meets legal frameworks in a straightforward and matter-of-fact way.

> 'But unless you embrace ambiguity and work out how to use the guidelines to guide you, not constrain you, you can't guarantee robust, safe accessibility practices. The further you get into the discipline, the more you understand that you need to create

knowledge of the specifics of the audience for accessibility – WCAG can only take you so far.

'While ambiguity and complexity might seem like things you'd wish to remove from a project, what I've found is that one of the joys of working in accessibility for a lot of developers is they find it challenging. It forces them to be creative. Good things don't have to be simple, as long as you've got a map to guide you.

'That's one of the interesting and useful parts of what BS 8878 (and ISO 30071-1) do: they give people a framework that allows them to negotiate ambiguous, difficult situations. In my view, accessibility should be about visionary people wanting to celebrate the diversity of their audiences in their products, not wanting to reduce that diversity to make product creation easier. I'm interested in what happens when we create products where the differences between the people using them are considered to be a strength rather than a weakness.'

d. Using your accessibility requirements to procure the product or outsource its creation

Most digital products are not created by the organisations that own them – organisations may outsource their production to specialist digital agencies, or procure a COTS product which satisfies most of their product requirements and customise it to include as many of the requirements as financially sensible. So the delivery of accessibility in your product is as likely to be impacted by clear communication of requirements between client and supplier in meetings and tender or contract documents as by conformance with technical accessibility guidelines. If you are procuring or outsourcing the creation of any aspect of your product and you get that communication wrong, the cost and effort to deliver an accessible product can sky-rocket. This final part of Activity 4 advises you on what to do to prevent that.

By this point, you'll have defined most aspects of the product you are creating and how you will uphold accessibility in it. You will have defined not only what your product should be, but also the level of accessibility quality that you are aiming for and some of the types of accessibility features you expect your product to provide. And you'll have captured all the functional and non-functional accessibility requirements, including success criteria linked to the level of accessibility experience you're aiming to deliver. This information will make it easier to ensure that the product will be accessible; whether you will create it from scratch or procure it; and whether you're going to do that in-house or outsource it to another organisation.

This is what makes ISO 30071-1 so valuable. It does not assume that organisations will develop their digital products themselves, and makes the link between accessible product development standards like WCAG and accessible product procurement standards like America's Section 508 Refresh[37] and EN 301 549.[38] Moreover, it enhances the checklist mentality of these standards with insights around assuring accessibility across multiple devices and social media channels.

All ISO 30071-1 activities are just as valid for either create or procure, but from this activity onwards, the way that you will make decisions will be fundamentally impacted by the choice you make now. If you decide that you're going to create the product from scratch in-house, then all of your decisions and work will continue to be up to you. If you really aren't going to procure any aspect of your product – even the use of third-party social media like Twitter, YouTube, Instagram or Facebook as additional communication channels to your website or mobile app – you can skip to the next activity.

If you're procuring all or part of the product – either from one COTS supplier and customising it to your needs, or by selecting and integrating multiple COTS products from more than one supplier – or outsourcing its creation to a supplier, you'll need to ensure:

- You're clear about the accessibility requirements for your product

- The supplier or COTS product you select is able to deliver those requirements

In my experience, the most intractable situations for delivering accessibility often happen in client-supplier relationships when the client is not clear about what accessibility they require, or completely forgets accessibility during procurement and only thinks of it after signing a contract with their supplier that doesn't mention accessibility at all.

Put in a nutshell: if you don't ask for accessibility, you don't get it.

How to use your ICT system accessibility log to aid successful procurement, outsourcing and supplier relations

If you're going down the procurement or outsourcing route, you'll be one step removed from ISO 30071-1's Activities 5 and 6 where the product design and development happen.

If you're *procuring* the product, its technology choices and adherence to technical accessibility guidelines (in this activity) and accessibility QA testing (see next activity) will have already been done (or not done). All you'll do is choose between a number of different products that claim to meet your accessibility requirements to a greater or lesser extent, and negotiate any product extension or modification necessary to bring it up to those requirements.

If you're *outsourcing* the development of your product to a supplier, you will input more strongly into the decisions they make in each of those activities by providing accessibility requirements for them to follow, but you'll also need to rely on the supplier to deliver to those requirements.

The way to get an accessible product via procurement or outsourcing is to be clear about your requirements. Thankfully, by this point, this is exactly what you've already written in your ICT system accessibility log and accessibility requirements.

Use that information to:

- Clearly specify the accessibility of the product that you wish to procure or contract suppliers to build in your *ITT or RFP documentation*

- Ensure accessibility is included in your *assessment of product features or supplier proposals* to choose the right COTS product or supplier to win your procurement or search for suppliers

- Clearly specify what accessibility you expect to be delivered by your chosen supplier in your *contract* with them

Embedding accessibility requirements in your procurement documentation and contracts

The prevalence of procurement and outsourcing in the creation of modern digital products is the reason why one of the first things my team does in our initial engagement with new clients is to encourage them to include an accessibility section in their standard ITT/RFP templates and procurement contracts (see Chapter 4 of this book's companion, *Inclusive Design for Organisations*). This accessibility section is a template specified in the organisation's general accessibility procurement policy, which is then filled out by the product manager with detailed information from the individual product's accessibility requirements.

As you've seen, using WCAG as a means for specifying your digital product's accessibility requirements always throws up many questions that are better answered by using ISO 30071-1's more user- and task-focused approach, specifying the product's accessibility requirements through:

- The tasks (Activity 2) that the product's target audiences (Activity 1) need to be able to complete

- The level of accessibility experience the product is aiming for (Activity 3)

- The devices, OSes, browsers and assistive technologies you've specified for the product to be used on (see Activities 1, 2 and 3)

- Any accessibility personalisation necessary to achieve this (see next activity)

This approach to specification is identical to what ISO 30071-1 recommends organisations that develop products themselves should do: specify successful delivery of accessibility via proof that the delivered product enables its target users to achieve what they came to it to achieve (the result), rather than proof the organisation has correctly followed a set of rules (the means) that may or may not have delivered that result.

At Hassell Inclusion, we also encourage our clients to be clear about their expectations for how suppliers should *prove* that they have met this level of accessibility experience when delivering the product for sign-off and launch, which draws from the discussion of the cost benefits of different types of accessibility test methodology in Activity 6.

Put in a nutshell: if you don't require your supplier to prove they've delivered accessibility, you don't know you've got it.

This more holistic specification of the accessibility requirements of the product (which often requires some form of user testing with disabled people as proof of the product's accessibility) is different from many organisations' current best practice, which is just to require conformance to a technical standard for accessibility such as WCAG 2.0 AA. That is, if they mention accessibility at all. My experience in outsourcing the creation of digital products (and I've personally commissioned digital products with a combined budget of approaching £10 million, and helped advise product managers handling accessibility in the outsourcing of hundreds more) is that the more specific you can be about exactly what you are *expecting* from your suppliers, the more likely they are to *deliver* what you are looking for, and the better the *relationship* will be between you and your supplier throughout the project.

ISO 30071-1's focus on what the COTS product or supplier needs to provide, in terms of the quality of the experience users will find when trying to complete tasks with the product, ensures that the product they deliver is fit for purpose for use by all the audiences you have specified. Whereas specifying accessibility against development guidelines like WCAG allows suppliers to deliver a product that meets the technical standard, but which disabled and older people may not be able to use to complete the tasks they came to the product to complete.

One of the major benefits found by organisations that integrate ISO 30071-1's activities into their production process is that, when their teams write their ITT and contract documentation, they are able to be very clear about what they expect, in terms of both accessibility and other aspects of the project. This clarity of expectations benefits both client and supplier.

How to select a supplier or COTS product that will deliver the accessibility you need

Being clear in specifying your requirements for how accessibility is to be delivered and assured by a supplier or COTS product is one half of the battle in successfully outsourcing or procuring an accessible digital product. The other half is being able to distinguish a supplier that is likely to deliver to your accessibility requirements, or a COTS product that can do so with the minimum of further modification or extension, from one that is not.

By specifying your accessibility requirements in terms of task completion by specified audiences to a specific level of accessibility experience across specified devices, OSes, browsers and assistive technologies, you are already marking yourself out as an organisation that cares about the accessibility experience of the product that you are creating for your target audiences, rather than being content with the risk mitigation of meeting technical accessibility standards like WCAG AA. But I'd recommend that your standard ITT wording should also require suppliers to specify *how* they will meet your product's specific accessibility requirements in their tender or proposal.

For *suppliers of COTS products,* this places the burden on them to prove their product meets your requirements, which pushes them beyond the usual claims of conformance with WCAG 2.0 AA or provision of accessibility conformance reports based on the Voluntary Product Accessibility Template®[39] that are often provided but are seldom independently verified. In meeting your ITT requirements, products that are suitable for upholding your accessibility aims will rise to the top.

For *suppliers of product development services,* this places the burden on them to prove to you that they have planned for and will assure the level of accessibility you require for the *specific product* you want them to create. My experience is that this in itself tends to separate those suppliers that can actually deliver accessibility from those that know the 'right answer' for accessibility is WCAG 2.0 AA, but don't necessarily understand what in practice is necessary to deliver a product that meets your accessibility aims.

To give an example of this, when I was commissioning e-learning games for the BBC in the mid-noughties, it was always clear which of our twenty-five preferred suppliers really understood what I was after, because they did much more than mention WCAG in their response to my ITT's questions on accessibility. At the time, the only web technology that could deliver the games that I needed was Adobe Flash, and Adobe Flash could not be made accessible using WCAG 1.0. Therefore, suppliers that simply quoted their WCAG conformance policy stood out as having missed the point and not engaged with the accessibility approach that was needed.

So if 'We create all our products to conform with WCAG 2.0 AA' isn't proof enough that a supplier can be relied on to deliver what you need, what proof is sufficient?

Here ISO 30071-1's activities help again, because what you need your suppliers to convince you of is that they have done a first draft version of all the work in Activities 5 and 6 in their preparation of their proposal:

- Any technology choices they've made in their proposal have taken accessibility into account (see Activity 5)

- Their development plan, testing plan, timescales and costs have taken accessibility into account (see Activity 6)

If you see *evidence* that the supplier has undertaken these activities in their proposal, you know not only that they have taken your accessibility requirements seriously, but also that the plans they have presented to you can be relied upon to deliver the accessibility you require. If you can't see this evidence, you are likely to get what usually happens, which is that suppliers forget accessibility until they test it late on in development, and they then argue that it needs to be downgraded because they haven't got any time left to rectify the accessibility flaws found in the testing.

Here's what Andrew Arch, Assistant Director, Web Policy – Accessibility for the Australian Government Information Management Office, had to say when I interviewed him:

'When the Australian government signed off the Web Accessibility National Transition Strategy requiring all sites to get to WCAG 2.0 AA, they probably thought, "We'll just change the colours and we'll change the font, job done." But it's much more complicated than that if you're relying on external suppliers of your systems. You may have an HR system, for instance, that does all your recruitment and HR management, and you've got a five-year contract, and it was delivered with minor accessibility in mind. People are going through procurement reviews and saying, "OK, when is this due for relicensing or renewal?" and saying to the big companies – international companies in many cases – "We need accessibility built into this." It's hard to do that after you've procured a system, so we've provided some advice to agencies around procurement from the start.

'Accessibility is not something that you check at the end of the process. You've got to make sure it's written into the requirements before you go to market so that the suppliers know that you're expecting it. Then you've got to check progressively, if they're building something, for instance, that they're actually doing it, because by the time it gets to the end, you've got to roll it out and you're not going to go back and fix it.

'[In the USA], I've heard anecdotes of organisations that have left accessibility until the end, met the business needs but not the accessibility needs. And the accounting and legal people said, "It's too hard, we're just going to have to wear it."

'Our [Australian] Human Rights Commission says, "If it's not accessible, it's not fit for use" and I like that phrase. You haven't purchased something that's actually fit for use if you haven't purchased something that's accessible and meets the needs of *all* users.'

The questions I've found that really separate suppliers who know what they are doing with accessibility from those who don't are:

• What elements of the product development are going to be most challenging for accessibility?

• How have you delivered accessibility on similar products that you've created in the past?

For suppliers of COTS products, I usually ask:

• What was your approach to accessibility when you created this product?

If your supplier lights up when you ask these questions and takes you through a great story, you're on to a winner. If they look uncomfortable and don't know how to reply, you know you'll have to tackle this head on should you plan to select them or their product.

What to do when no supplier can meet your accessibility requirements

The establishing of strong procurement requirements in US and European standards is encouraging suppliers of enabling technologies, COTS products and product creation services to take accessibility seriously, but there can still be situations when you may not be able to find a supplier or COTS product that can deliver the level of accessibility experience you need. In these cases, ISO 30071-1 recognises that it may be necessary for organisations to procure products that do not deliver the desired level of accessibility experience, as long as they are making an *informed* decision that balances accessibility risk against other business needs.

In these circumstances, your contract negotiation should include discussions with the supplier to see if they will put accessibility improvements on their roadmap (using the business cases for accessibility from Chapter 3 in this book's companion, *Inclusive Design for Organisations*, as leverage) and what alternative measures need to be put in place for users who are affected by the product's accessibility deficiencies (at a minimum, declaring the deficiencies in the product's accessibility statement – see Activity 7).

Remediation of products where accessibility requirements were not part of your contract with your supplier

The real-world worst-case scenario for delivering accessible products is where you wish to improve the accessibility of a product or service that you've just procured from an external supplier, but you didn't mention accessibility at all in the contract. In these circumstances, you as the purchaser do not have any legal leverage to require your supplier to improve the accessibility of their product, at least until a break clause in the contract.

My team has helped many organisations through these circumstances by:

- Testing the product to find its accessibility deficiencies

- Leading negotiation exercises to go through the list of deficiencies, estimating the benefits to the organisation and costs to the supplier that

would come from fixing each issue, to come to
a prioritised list of which issues could be most
usefully fixed in the short term (see the section
on the Accessibility Issue Prioritisation Matrix in
Activity 6)

The issue of who should pay for those fixes is
a contentious one, and the only leverage the
organisation usually has is based on what they
could require from the supplier to not terminate the
contract at the next break clause. But you may gain
some more leverage by introducing the supplier
to the sales benefits of improving their product's
accessibility (see Chapter 3 in this book's companion,
Inclusive Design for Organisations) if they aren't aware
of them.

Whatever the final result, this sort of exercise
provides a useful framework for both client and
supplier to work through the issues to come to the
best conclusion they can agree on for how to proceed,
and at Hassell Inclusion, we have got good results
and feedback from both clients and suppliers after
conducting it.

How ISO 30071-1 can protect client-supplier relationships by aligning expectations

Once you have chosen a supplier, it is a good idea to get the supplier into a workshop to work together with your organisation to plan the accessibility on a product's implementation in more detail, using ISO 30071-1 as a framework for discussing the necessary issues. Taking care to align and document the expectations of client and supplier for how accessibility requirements will be met (see Activity 6) at the start of the outsourcing or COTS product customisation project may take time but can pay massive dividends as development proceeds as both sides know they are aiming for the same thing. This results in accessible products created through transparent dialogue, not disputes, which tend to arise when delivered products are found to not meet client aims far too late in the process for accessibility to be delivered with reasonable cost.

For an example of the benefits of doing this on large multi-supplier projects, see Rob Wemyss's case study on the use of BS 8878 from when he was Head of Accessibility at Royal Mail.[40]

ISO 30071-1 procurement requirements raising the accessibility bar for suppliers

Finally, one interesting impact of ISO 30071-1 on the market for accessible products is that it encourages commissioners of outsourced digital products and procurers of COTS products to think more deeply about what they expect from the accessibility of products. This helps suppliers that are competent in delivering accessibility, or are willing to step up to the challenge contractually, to differentiate themselves from those that aren't, and win more business.

In essence, if you are a supplier, ISO 30071-1 gives you a better business case for improving your competence at delivering accessibility and selling it as one of your USPs. As you see evidence in ITTs that companies commissioning your work care about accessibility and value this USP, you will be able to be more transparent about including the actual costs of accessibility in proposals, and not feel that by pitching these slightly higher costs you will lose business to competitors that pitch lower charges for inaccessible products. And if you are a COTS vendor and you follow ISO 30071-1 in your product's development, this will give you everything you need to convince customers that are also following ISO 30071-1 that your product meets their accessibility requirements, both at the time of procurement and in an ongoing way.

While Section 508 Refresh in the United States and EN 301 549 in Europe do a good job of requiring IT product procurement to take accessibility into account in public-sector organisations, ISO 30071-1 raises the bar for private-sector companies too.

NOW IT'S YOUR TURN

- Use the ICT system accessibility log template to guide you through choosing the implementation technologies, guidelines and enabling technologies that you will use to build your product. Consider how accessibility is supported in all the social media channels you plan to use to communicate with your audiences and create strategies for getting around any accessibility deficiencies in those channels.

- If you are going to use any procured components in your product, or outsource its creation to an external supplier, note this in your digital product's ICT service accessibility log.

- Download and use the ITT templates in the support materials for this book (see the 'Support materials to accompany this book' section at the beginning) as a guide to specify what accessibility you will require from any components, products or services you purchase.

ACTIVITY 5

Specify Design Approach

'I don't want "design for all", I want "design for me".'

Activity 5 is all about how to design your product in relation to the accessibility ecosystem on the device. Each level (if it's available) can allow people to customise the user experience of your product so it better suits their needs. But there are limits to these inclusive or universal design approaches to accessibility. So on occasion, you may also need to provide user-personalised/individualised approaches.

There are two types of situations when this may be needed:

- When groups of users have contradictory needs and preferences

- When the context of use of the product means that elements of the accessibility ecosystem that usually facilitate accessibility are not available

To introduce it, let me tell you a story:

During my time at the BBC, my team received a number of accessibility comments on the update of the BBC News website in July 2010. One comment said:

'Terrible contrast between the grey text and dark background.'

Nineteen minutes later, we received this comment:

'The background colour is forced to white high contrast – contributes to eyestrain and headaches. Perhaps a light grey would help here.'

Both of these users had difficulty with reading text in the colours used on the site. WCAG 2.0 AA success criteria support the needs of the first person, but if the site had followed WCAG's colour-contrast success criteria even more strongly than it had already done to help the person who made the first comment, it would have become even harder to use for the person who made the second comment who wanted less contrast between the foreground and background colours.

Doing user research into this conundrum, my team and I found that there were as many people who wanted less contrast because of dyslexia or other literacy difficulties as people who wanted more contrast between foreground and background colour because of vision impairments. Here the WCAG AA colour-contrast success criterion didn't help us get what we needed, which was to give both sets of users a good user experience. There was a AAA success criterion that mentioned enabling users to select foreground and background colours, but like most organisations, AAA success criteria weren't part of our accessibility guidelines.

If you were in that circumstance, what would you do?

In this case, I wrote back to both users, letting them know that there were controls in their browsers that could help them override the colours that we had chosen for the website to replace them with the colours they wanted, referencing the award-winning website My Web My Way[1] that I'd commissioned in 2006 to document how people could use the accessibility settings in their OS and browser to customise their web experience. However, through conversation with them, I found that providing information wasn't enough. Even though they were now aware of the controls in their browsers, they were scared of using them. The solution I had provided did not work for them because they weren't confident enough in their technical abilities to do what was required of them.

At this point, the BBC's motivation for caring about accessibility was key. If the BBC had cared about accessibility purely from a risk-mitigation viewpoint, then this example would end here as the BBC could be confident that it would have mitigated its risk by following WCAG 2.0 AA. However, the BBC's motivation for accessibility was based on aiming to ensure that as many licence-fee payers could use its products as reasonably possible. Therefore, we needed to go beyond the guidelines to find solutions that really worked for our users.

The resulting user research, both qualitative in labs with real people and quantitative desk research, found that there were a large number of people experiencing similar difficulties because of the lack of accessibility personalisation features on the BBC site.[2] Using this research, I was able to create a business case based on the number of people encountering these difficulties and the impact of those difficulties on their use of our site to fund the creation of a prototype to investigate how we could help them.

The prototype BBC Preferences System, or MyDisplay as it was called, gained quite a few users and won its own awards,[3] but the BBC wasn't in a position to do the thing its users really wanted, which was to make it available on all websites. As this would have been outside the BBC's remit as a broadcaster, it decided it wasn't able to take it further.

A few years later, after I'd left the BBC, I was able to extend the research with support from the Technology Strategy Board and develop a new cloud-based accessibility personalisation tool with a completely revised architecture and coding. This tool can now add accessibility personalisation to any website.[4]

This is an example of the limitations of the non-individualised 'single-design' approach to accessibility, which is the one commonly used in the digital industry. The aim is to create one website or app that, through the right use of guidelines like WCAG, can be transformed to the user's needs by their assistive technology or use of browser or OS accessibility preferences. This approach – where users provide the assistive technologies to help their needs – works well for product owners, so always consider it first on all digital projects. But more is sometimes needed.

a. Your options when a single-design approach doesn't work

As the example above highlights, not all users have the assistive technologies they need to make an inclusively designed digital product work for them. But WCAG is like the 20-tonne behemoth of accessibility. It's fabulous when it's helping you, but the strictness of its rules may crush you if you haven't found out enough about the reasons for those rules, how to sensibly apply them, and when it is justifiable to go beyond its rules. Thankfully, this is one of the strengths of following the ISO 30071-1 activities: by the time you arrive at the technical guidance WCAG gives, you've already established the strategic grounding for making sensible technical decisions about how you're going to deliver accessibility for your product, based on justifiable reasoning.

There may also be occasions where different groups of users need different things from a website or app, which no assistive technology exists to facilitate.

For example, people with learning difficulties benefit from products that are as simple as possible. These products may even dispense with providing the product's non-core goals to provide an interface that is optimised to access the core goals. The users' needs, in this respect, are completely at odds with the needs of the product manager who, like every other product manager, wants more functionality to show off in new versions of the product.

Similarly, different users of a video on a website may want completely different versions: blind and partially sighted people want an audio-described version; people who are hard of hearing will want captions; and people who use sign language will want a sign-interpreted version.

Educationalists have established that people learn in different ways, so e-learning sites give people a number of options – learning through reading, watching, building or playing – that are based around their different learning styles. Inspired by this, ISO 30071-1 takes the standard single-design approach and adds two optional user-personalised/ individualised approaches for providing accessibility:

- To create *multiple alternate versions* of part of the product (or the whole product), each of which has the same purpose but is personalised to the needs of specific members of the target audiences

- To embed the ability for that one digital product to be *personalised* to the needs of specific members of its target audience

Technical accessibility guidelines like WCAG, which generally take a single-design view, recognise user-personalised approaches and may summarise them under the heading of 'additional accessibility measures'.

Quite correctly, WCAG advises that these additional accessibility measures should *always complement* and *never replace* inclusive design approaches. And ISO 30071-1 advises that you set boundaries around what user needs you will respond to via user-personalised/individualised approaches, based on the *reasonableness* of the costs of responding to those user needs.

Multiple alternate versions

The original idea of additional accessibility measures was a response to a time when assistive technologies like screen readers weren't able to handle plug-in content like Adobe Flash, so WCAG required product owners to provide people with disabilities with 'HTML alternatives' to that content, assuming that was possible. The need for these alternative versions due to the choice of technology is now less common with the introduction and widespread usage of HTML 5, but alternative versions to meet the needs of different users still make sense where user research has suggested that different users would be better supported by significantly different sets of interactions or content – ie where the 'one-size-fits-all' approach doesn't work.

For an example of a situation where different alternative versions were necessary, this is from my interview with my regular collaborator, Martin Wright of Gamelab UK:

'When I saw your ITT for e-learning games to help deaf children with reading and writing, I said, "This is the one for us." I'd worked with deaf students. I'd understood the cultural differences and where deaf people were coming from. Where literacy is taught coherently, it is very much phonic based.

'I also understood that British Sign Language is not just an extension of English, it's a language in its own right. It has its own grammar and semantics and so on. We had to go beyond inclusion – if we were going to create a literacy product that worked for everybody, we needed to understand their context. We couldn't just say, "Let's just add a few BSL videos to our standard product."

'In the end we picked up a piece of technology that had been used in the Post Office – 3D signing avatars. We had to adapt that into a cartoon context, and immediately applying this clever technology to a game space was powerful.'

The huge unmet need for text personalisation

ISO 30071-1 agrees that a single inclusive design is always the best start, but it also recognises that, unlike the non-digital product world where personalisation is difficult and inclusive design is often the only way of creating a product that can be used by the widest audience, software personalisation is something that is comparatively easy, and is something that modern users have become conditioned to expect (see Activity 1).

One example of this type of personalisation is the 'style switcher' accessibility preference tools some websites and apps include to allow the user to personalise the text font, text size or spacing, or change text and background colours – as recommended by the WCAG 2.0 AAA success criterion I mentioned earlier[5] and the new WCAG 2.1 AA text spacing success criterion 1.4.12.[6]

Much of this personalisation is already available in the accessibility preferences set in browsers or OSes on desktop or laptop computers, or via browser plugins for people who are happy to install them (this does *not* include older people, who user research found weren't happy to do this sort of installation). But they provide a simpler interface to the functionality for the great majority of users who aren't technical. They are also independent of the accessibility features of the user's OS and browser, which can be exceptionally useful as mobile browsers commonly omit these features.

The importance of the unmet need for text personalisation (or customisation) facilities, whether in the product, OS or browser, is becoming more recognised after research by Shawn Henry and myself.[7] Here's what Shawn, accessibility evangelist and author of *Just Ask*, said when I interviewed her about her TAdER project[8]:

'I was needing text customisation to read websites, PDF documents and other electronic text. In some situations it was easy to make the text work and in others it wasn't – text customisation was just not available. There wasn't functionality in the products. And when I spoke with product managers, they said, "Well we don't hear a lot of people saying they need this."

'When I managed to convince some, they said, "So what do we need to do?" And I found that there wasn't a good resource to point them to…

'The project started by gathering stories, experiences and information so that we could show the need for text customisation. I was so surprised at the range of issues – nausea, dizziness, severe pain, confusion, inability to read – that I had to ask people for permission to publish their actual responses.

'If you provide electronic content in a way that users can't customise, you're causing these reactions. Reading your content is hurting people. And it's hurting you, because you want people to have a good experience.

The statistics are on the site. And some are surprising.

'We often focus on accessibility for people who are blind, and certainly it's absolutely necessary. But there's over seven times more people with low vision than who are blind. And some estimates say 15–20% of the population have symptoms of dyslexia. And there's a lot of people who are ageing but don't want to admit that they might need accommodations, don't even realise that they are possible. When I showed my father how to increase text size in his browser, he was thrilled. He didn't even know to ask for it.'

b. Situations where accessibility via the accessibility ecosystem isn't available

Text personalisation is just one example of a situation where parts of the ecosystem that are supposed to support user-personalisation aren't working because of the context of use of your product. In the example at the start of the chapter, the browser settings were available to help the users, but they weren't aware of them or couldn't get them to work. They needed something simpler. In Shawn's example, some technologies enabled personalisation (websites on desktop browsers) and others did not (websites on mobile browsers and PDF documents in PDF readers). She needed something more consistent.

These are not the only situations when the ecosystem breaks down. Most sets of guidelines, like WCAG, depend on assistive technologies, browser settings or accessibility settings in the OS being available to make the correctly coded product accessible to the user. Where they are not, if the organisation is looking to deliver an effective and efficient level of accessibility experience, it will need to find other ways of delivering this.

Here are some situations when this may be necessary:

- **No assistive technologies available:** where people with disabilities in the target audiences are in parts of the world where assistive technologies don't support their needs – for example, if they speak Arabic and there is no Arabic text-to-speech synthesiser available for their screen reader. David Banes sorted this out for Arabic during his time at MADA (see my extended interview with him in this book's supporting materials), and Apple and Google are doing a good job with supporting increasing numbers of languages in screen readers on iOS and Android, but there are still languages which aren't supported.

- **No awareness or ability to get assistive technologies onto the device:** where disabled people in the target audiences aren't aware that the assistive technologies exist, or can't afford them or access help to install them. This is particularly the case in the Developing World, as we discussed in Activity 2.

- **The device is shared so settings are locked-down.** If the device the digital product is on is shared – for example, it could be a sales kiosk in a shop, a ticket kiosk in an airport, a shared interactive screen in a museum or an in-flight entertainment system – many of these embedded devices won't support assistive technologies. Even if the device does supports assistive technologies (for example, it is an embedded Android tablet), it is likely that it will be locked into displaying the app so it's not possible to change its accessibility settings.

User-personalised solutions for these scenarios are based on the idea of a 'second personalised screen' where devices without accessibility support are able to be controlled by the user's own personal mobile device. For example:

- **No assistive technologies available.** If your
  cheap e-reader doesn't have text to speech
  because of the excessive bill of materials (BOM)
  costs of text-to-speech synthesiser licences, your
  mobile device is likely to have an app to read the
  same eBooks.

  Games companies like Nintendo[9] are also
  starting to use mobile apps to provide accessible
  channels for voice communications between
  players, which the consoles themselves cannot
  make accessible.

- **Where the device is shared so settings are
  locked-down.** While providing access to
  accessibility settings from within the app is
  possible, this would then require a disabled user
  (or staff member) to turn on the settings to use
  them and remember to turn them off before the
  next person uses the device. I'd recommend that
  you allow people to access the shared device
  (kiosk) service through their own mobile device.

  If the shared device's app can be run on the
  user's device, making it accessible is as easy as
  making your usual mobile app accessible, other
  than interfacing with the purchasing mechanism,
  ticket printing mechanism or in-flight
  entertainment media server that the app is
  controlling. Not only does the user have assistive

technologies on the device that they can turn on, but they will already have all the assistive technology settings set to their preferences.

This could also work for kiosks that have no assistive technologies, like ATMs. The UI on the ATM doesn't need to be the sole way of interfacing with the money dispenser. If the user can use the bank's mobile banking app on their mobile device as the ATM UI while they are in the queue, they can use it with their assistive technologies and accessibility settings, and they could then place their device on a near-field-communication sensor on the ATM to dispense the money when they reach the front of the queue. Assuming this was secure for the banks, this would be more accessible for people with disabilities, cheaper than trying to create assistive technologies for ATMs, and would speed up ATM queues for everyone.

This second personalised screen concept is already working for in-flight entertainment on some airlines. It would cost millions to add assistive technologies and accessibility settings to these seat-back screens and they still wouldn't be easily reachable for people with motor impairments, but enable access to the entertainment via a UI on the user's tablet or smartphone and everything works for everyone.

The concept can also work for shared big screens in stadiums, theme parks, museums and galleries. The problem with putting captions, AD or signing on video on big screens for those who need them is that many people get distracted by these access services if they don't need them. Allowing streaming of what's on the screen to the personal device in your hands gets around this problem. Everyone can then get the access services that they need.

These personal handheld screens are already available in some places, for example at the Barça Stadium Tour & Museum at Barcelona's football ground, Camp Nou.[10] And tablets and smart glasses are being trialled to bring captions and AD to cinemas and theatres, for example at the National Theatre in London.[11]

I see the opportunities in moving from mobile to wearables (smart watches strapped to my wrist, smart glasses that I wear), and possible future advances in smart contact lenses and brain-machine interfaces as key to extending this personalised control of digital devices in the user's environment even further. With 5G, it truly could be the *inclusive* Internet of Things.

NOW IT'S YOUR TURN

- Use the ICT system accessibility log template to guide you through considering whether it would make sense to add user-personalised approaches to accessibility to your inclusive design model

- If you think you might need to create product variants, I'd recommend you read my blogs on 'Beyond inclusion and reverse inclusion'[12] for inspiration on when to do it, how to do it and the innovation opportunities that can come from it

Ensure Accessibility Requirements Are Met

This activity is about developing your digital product using the decisions you made in the previous five activities to guide you. It's about understanding the impact on accessibility of the large numbers of technical decisions your product team will make as they develop the product day by day. And it's about easing the commonly experienced stress of having to deal with lots of accessibility issues just before launch by:

- Planning to deliver accessibility in each stage of development

- Planning to test for accessibility throughout development

- Planning for communicating accessibility decisions in the product's launch

The other key concept here is *prioritisation*. If you find during development and testing that you cannot deliver all of the accessibility aims you have planned for, or fix all the issues that your testing has found, it's about using cost-benefits analyses to help make justifiable decisions. These will help you decide which aspects of the product's accessibility are most important and should be prioritised, and which aspects are less important and could be sacrificed if necessary to deliver your product on time and to budget. Throughout, we will use a key tool that will help you do this prioritisation – the *Accessibility Issue Prioritisation Matrix* that has helped so many Hassell Inclusion clients.

a. Assure the product's accessibility through implementation planning

Now you've established which technical accessibility guidelines are appropriate for use in your product's development as part of your accessibility requirements and a sensible attitude to exceptions which don't feel appropriate, you can start to use them well.

Accessibility guidelines are regularly used by many of the people on product development teams to guide their work, but one role that often gets missed out is the *project manager* who is responsible for planning the use of resources across the project. The project manager needs to know how to plan accessibility work across the length of the project for the activities of the different people working on it to come together to deliver a product that achieves its accessibility goals. Thankfully, the project manager has as much to gain from using accessibility guidelines as every other member of the team.

Used well, they help the project manager to:

• Break down accessibility aims for the product into the decisions they need to make to uphold those aims on a more granular level

• Estimate the time needed to deliver accessibility on each aspect of the project

While ISO 30071-1's activities can be integrated into Waterfall development processes, I'm going to assume that your organisation – like most of the digital industry – will be using some form of Agile methodology to project manage your product's development. So I'm going to use the language of 'product backlogs', 'user stories', 'story points' and 'sprints' here. For those who aren't using Scrum yet, the definition of all these terms, along with why Agile makes sense for digital project management, can be found in Wikipedia's article on Scrum (software development).[1]

From an Agile project planning perspective, accessibility requirements break down into two distinct groups:

- A lot of quality guidelines requiring you to embed accessibility *as a testable quality into each existing user story* in your product backlog, documented in something like Jira[2] or Trello[3], and providing implementation techniques and success criteria against which you can test that quality (eg implementing designs with the right semantics, so headings are enclosed in heading tags rather than just marked as bold)

- A few functionality guidelines requiring you to add *accessibility-specific user stories* into your product backlog (eg including a 'style switcher' tool to enable the user to change the colours of your product to their preferred style)

Make sure your scheduling of the implementation of each user story uses the accessibility requirements to:

- Help you define and document what accessibility *success* for the user story means

- Help your team members *estimate how long* it will take them to deliver the feature with the level of accessibility quality required by the guideline (alongside other code qualities like performance, robustness or security, or design qualities like simplicity, usability or aesthetics)

And make sure you schedule the implementation of any accessibility-specific user stories you need to include to meet the accessibility requirements.

Doing this ensures the 'development overhead' for implementing accessibility is embedded throughout your product backlog, rather than tacked on at the end of your development as an after-the-fact remediation exercise in fixing accessibility defects you could have avoided creating in the first place. It ensures accessibility isn't forgotten, and is an efficient way of including accessibility across the development, testing and fixing parts of your project.

Ideally, when you're splitting your backlog into sprints, any user stories which are particularly challenging to get right from an accessibility point of view would be put early in your implementation plan. After all, good project managers do risky tasks first.[4] Asking your developers, 'What do you think are going to be the hardest parts of our product to make accessible?' could bring you real dividends.

Documenting and implementing your product's accessibility requirements

Satisfying accessibility requirements in your development of user stories is relatively straightforward if you have broken down your technical accessibility guideline's checkpoints (eg WCAG success criteria) by job role, and assessed and trained all of your team to be accessibility competent and confident as I suggest in Chapter 4 of this book's companion, *Inclusive Design for Organisations*. With this done, each team member should have a shortlist of success criteria to watch out for. If you *have assessed and trust their accessibility competence and confidence*, it should be sufficient to mention that the guidelines need to be applied across all user stories in an Epic. If you haven't, mention the appropriate accessibility requirements for each user story on its Jira card.

Each team member should use best-practice accessible design or code patterns (such as WCAG's techniques for each success criterion) whenever they create a new element of design, code or content, or check that the accessibility patterns have been implemented in elements they are selecting, modifying and incorporating from code libraries or style guides. If it's easy to implement accessible techniques as planned, your team should do so. If it isn't as easy as they estimated in the planning process and continuing to work to find an accessible solution will cause delays in delivery or an increase in resource costs, they should do the necessary cost-benefits analysis to make an informed exception request (see Activity 4). The project manager and product manager should review the exception request and decide if the project sprint planning can flex to accommodate the extra resource or time needed, or whether to accept the exception and downgrade the accessibility of the user story.

How to make accessibility decisions when things don't go to plan

Once you've set your plan to deliver the level of accessibility experience you are aiming for, monitor your team's progress against that delivery as the project's development progresses. For this purpose, the documentation of each development decision is critical for exposing the costs and risks in making justifiable exception decisions.

Often, the work you do to make something accessible doesn't deliver the accessibility you were aiming for when you test it (see later in this activity for how to plan that testing), and there's not enough time in the schedule to fix it due to conflicting product requirements. The project may also fall behind in its implementation plan, which can create pressure to make decisions to downgrade the accessibility requirements of some user stories to catch up. Where exception requests claim this is needed, the understanding of which of the product's user goals are core and which are non-core can aid your prioritisation. Do what you can to protect the delivery of accessible core user goals and take resource from delivering the accessibility of non-core user goals if you need it.

Whatever the reasoning behind exception requests, it is essential for your accessibility decision documentation to give two groups of people the information they need to make informed decisions.

Firstly, the product and project managers need to be able to quickly review the *cumulative impact* of each accessibility decision made on the accessibility experience, budget and risk profile of the product. They also need to be able to see any relationships between decisions – how one decision has prompted others, or where a request is being made that undercuts previous decisions (for example, where a project has already created or procured a media player that can play captioned video, but then a decision is made to not caption any of the video). This will enable them to make informed decisions in the context of the impact of previous decisions as well as the fit with the accessibility aims of the product. There is a trade-off between denying or accepting the exception request, so they either accept the resource cost of requiring the implementation of an accessibility technique, or save the resource cost and incur the accessibility risk that comes from not implementing the technique.

The product and project managers need some form of dashboard to be able to quickly review how each decision impacts the whole project's accessibility experience, budget and risk, as this is the key way of assessing the justification for each decision and tracking the accessibility profile of the product as it develops.

Secondly, other team members need to be able to access the *detail of strategic research and decisions made in previous activities* to provide firm grounding for their exception requests.

Your ideal accessibility documentation management system should support both of these needs, with some form of dashboard showing:

- Current levels of accessibility experience, budget and risk

- High-level summaries of how many exception decisions are being made, where they're being made and what sort of decisions they are

- Notifications of key decisions that have most impact on the accessibility of the product

- A mechanism for allowing the whole team to drill down into detail where they wish to take a closer look

The system needs to be available wherever decisions are made. And it needs to be lightweight so it doesn't take long to document exception decisions once they are made to minimise this overhead on the project's progress. Ideally, your documentation for accessibility decisions in this activity should be integrated into the documentation system for other (non-accessibility) decisions in the rest of the project – the product's Jira or Confluence[5] page. This will allow accessibility decisions to be made in the context of all the other decisions, priorities and pressures on that aspect and the rest of the project.

The higher-level ICT system accessibility log document could be part of the same system, or be a separate living document that links to the project documentation system for detailed decisions in this activity. Either way, the decisions summarised in the document – especially the documentation of exceptions that will result in *accessibility deficiencies* in the final product you deliver – will be a key resource to use later in this activity for assessing how much accessibility risk you will incur when you launch the product, creating an ICT system accessibility statement to communicate those deficiencies to your users, and planning to fix any of those deficiencies post-launch.

NOW IT'S YOUR TURN

- To get your development started on the right foot, use the web accessibility development planning template in the book's support materials to guide you in holding a workshop to plan accessibility into your project backlog.

- Tools to integrate ISO 30071-1-style accessibility decisions into popular Agile project management systems like Jira are currently being investigated. If you're interested, sign up for ISO 30071-1 tool updates when downloading the support materials for this book.

b. Assure the product's accessibility through testing

Testing is the first thing organisations think of when they wake up to the need to make their products accessible. More money is spent on accessibility testing than any other aspect of accessibility work. And unfortunately, because organisations don't often plan their accessibility testing strategically, much of that money is wasted.

Here, I'll show you how to minimise your testing spend and maximise its value to your product.

You've already set the accessibility requirements of the product and you've chosen technical accessibility guidelines to advise each member of your development team on what to do to create each aspect of the product in a way that can be tested to see if it meets those requirements. To use an analogy from the motor industry, this is like the specification sheet of a car.

But how do you know if the combined effect of the team's good intentions will actually result in a product that upholds your accessibility aims – to give your users the technical, effective and efficient, or satisfying level of accessibility experience that you'd like them to get from your product? To continue the analogy, no one buys a car based on reading its specification sheet – they buy it based on a test drive.

So there are multiple ways to test your product's accessibility, and many times at which you can do this testing – not just right before launch.

Why accessibility testing needs to be part of the product's test plan

There's nothing unusual about the desire to test a product as you are creating it. You're already likely to be doing unit testing, integration testing, QA testing, some form of usability or customer experience testing with users pre-launch, and combinations of all of these with regression testing post-launch. You'll probably have put together a *test plan* specifying which types of testing to use at which stages of development to strategically tell you whether the product is developing in the right direction and upholding your quality goals. The reason you do this multi-stage, multi-methodology testing is because it's essential to find bugs *as early as possible* in development, as the cost of fixing bugs depends on when you find them.

So why do most organisations leave accessibility testing to *the very end* of the project when it will be expensive to fix problems, most of which could have been found much earlier? And why do they only use one accessibility testing methodology – auditing against WCAG – when many others are also available that are more reliable for evaluating whether or not the product is accessible and usable for disabled users?

To avoid wasting time and money in this way, incorporate testing for accessibility into *each* stage of the product's test plan, using the accessibility testing methodology that is most appropriate for the type of product you are creating at the stage of development you have reached, to maximise testing benefits and minimise fixing costs. If this extra testing sounds expensive, the good news is that integrating accessibility testing into the test plans you already have rather than doing it on its own can make it cheaper than you may think.

Here's an example of how integrating accessibility and usability testing can pay major dividends from my interview with Andrew Arch, Assistant Director, Web Policy – Accessibility for the Australian Government Information Management Office:

> 'The general usability that people talk about is equally important for people with disabilities: 20% of the population has a disability. Do

20% of the users that you're doing usability studies with for your new product have a disability? In Japan by the end of this decade [the 2010s], 35% of people will be over sixty-five. That means that one-third of your users in Japan included in usability studies should potentially be older people.

'If your target audience is everybody, which it is for most government information or banking sites, when you're building personas to act as truth checkers internally as you go through, people with disabilities and older people need to be part of that mix.

'It's really noticeable now that the better usability companies are saying, "Accessibility is part of our responsibility as well." They've got pure user experience experts and some accessibility experts. But it's where they're working together in teams that we're getting the best results. Because the great thing is, the usability companies that do include people with disabilities find just as many, if not more, usability issues because it's more important for people with disabilities.'

It shouldn't come as too much of a surprise to hear that it is useful to harmonise accessibility testing with usability testing. ISO 30071-1 encourages you to aim to create a product that is usable to all of its different audiences through your accessibility strategy. Disabled people are just one audience for usability alongside people who, as some disabled people say with a hint of irony, 'Haven't become disabled yet'. My experience at the BBC was that bringing together user testing of products with disabled people and user testing of products with non-disabled people can save up to 40% of the combined costs of both.

Of course, user testing is only one testing methodology, and not all of the benefits mentioned in the interview would necessarily have been available if the testing had been done earlier in the development process. But these sorts of cost savings at least indicate that it's worth looking closely at different accessibility testing methodologies and whether they can be incorporated into other 'mainstream' testing methodologies.

A summary of accessibility testing methodologies

There are many ways of testing the accessibility of a digital product. To continue the motor industry analogy from earlier, some are about testing the 'specification sheet' (whether the product has been built in the right way), and others are about going for a 'test drive' (whether the product provides a user experience that users would want to repeat).

To summarise methodologies in each of these categories:

- 'Specification sheet' tests:

  - You could test conformance to the technical accessibility guidelines you'll have chosen in Activity 4, either manually or via software automation

- 'Test-drive' tests:

  - You could put the product in front of its target users, either face to face in a lab or in the context in which the product will be most used, or remotely using user-testing software, and see whether they can complete the user tasks that you specified in Activity 2 without any prompting or help

  - To save money, you could get accessibility experts to do 'cognitive walkthroughs' of those user tasks, acting as if they had the different impairments of your target users to see if they uncover any barriers to achieving the definition of success for each user task

– You could check that the user experience and behaviour of your product is consistent against the set of different browsers and assistive technologies your target audiences may use (as you specified in Activity 3)

Each of these methodologies may have different costs and different strengths and weaknesses for producing reliable, actionable findings (see the figure below). Each may also have a particular point in the development process where it is best used.

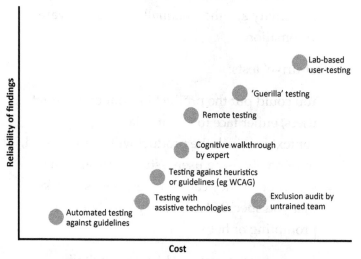

Cost benefits of different types of accessibility testing

ISO 30071-1 advises that it is most efficient if you use a combination of these methodologies to test the accessibility of your product, depending on the level of accessibility experience you are aiming for. So let's examine each of the accessibility testing methodologies and where to consider including them in your testing plan.

'Specification sheet' tests – manual and automated heuristic testing

Testing your product against success criteria in the accessibility guidelines that you chose in Activity 4 (such as WCAG) is the most common current form of accessibility testing. It looks for the presence of issues that are likely to cause barriers for people with disabilities to use pages of your site, or screens in your app.

Your QA team should test the accessibility of each team member's work, but it should also be each team member's responsibility, after the right training and with the right tools, to check their own work on a product to ensure it conforms with each success criterion for their job role before passing it on to other members of the team to progress through development. For example:

- Interaction designers should check the accessibility of the information structure in their wireframes before passing them on to visual designers

- Visual designers should check the accessibility of their use of colour, typography and images when adding the 'style and look' to the wireframe before they pass their designs to client-side coders

- Coders should check the accessibility of their page templates – that they've coded the semantics of the design as well as the look of it, and provided flexibility for text resizing etc – before passing them on to content authors

- Content authors should check their content is written in simple language and images have alt-text

The value of this is worth highlighting:

- Each bug found early by team members or QA testers during design and development will be much cheaper to fix than each bug found in pre-launch audits.

- Automated tools can and should be used to help this heuristic testing. They are not sufficient on their own – they can only reliably test a subset of about 20–30% of WCAG – but it makes perfect sense to use them for their strengths. Automate whatever can be automated, so you can concentrate time and effort on finding the things that can only be found by manual testing.

Here's a guide to where to use heuristic testing during your development. At each point, I'll identify examples of what your team members or QA teams need to consider to do this testing well:

- What tools are available to help them complete the testing quickly and easily

- Which of the guidelines these tools will help them test

- Where automated tests can produce reliable findings

- Where extra manual testing is needed

Testing the accessibility of initial wireframes and visual designs

Firstly, test initial wireframes and visuals against success criteria for interaction and visual designers in the technical accessibility guidelines you chose. No automated tools exist that can do this for designs, so do this manually and fix any accessibility defects before they're implemented in code.

Tools can be useful in making this testing more efficient, for example:

- For checking colour combinations used in visual design, many free colour-contrast tools are available, for example from WebAIM[6] or Tanaguru[7]

Once initial designs are implemented in code, your teams can use other tools to double-check their accessibility. For example:

- For checking that the order of content is logical on a web page, you could use the free aDesigner tool[8] to visualise the length of time it takes to get to portions of the page when listening via a screen reader

- For checking that the visual structure of the page does not break when text is resized to 200%, you could use the text-resizing functionality of your browser (see My Web My Way for details of how to access this functionality in different browsers[9])

Unit and integration testing of code accessibility

During development, continuous integration testing of the code in the product's page or screen templates and components should include testing against the success criteria for client-side developers in your technical accessibility guidelines. Fix any accessibility defects before content is added to those templates.

Tools can be useful in making this testing more efficient, for example:

- For checking the presence of alt-text, labelling of form controls, and accessibility properties set on elements of a web page, you could use the free WAVE toolbar,[10] automated tools from numerous software vendors[11] or integration of accessibility unit test libraries like axe[12] into continuous integration (CI) testing frameworks like Selenium or Appium

- For checking that a page's mark-up is structured correctly, QA testers can use the tab and enter keys to manually navigate the page as a keyboard user

Testing of content accessibility

The content in the product should be manually tested against the success criteria for content authors in your technical accessibility guidelines and any accessibility defects fixed. Automated tools can be helpful in testing large numbers of pages for some simple content accessibility defects like the absence of alt-text for an image or a title for a page, but they cannot check against all guidelines. For example, the only way of checking whether the alt-text for an image or title for a page is meaningful is to review it manually.

Pre-launch accessibility audits

To reduce the legal risk from launching a product without knowledge of its quality of accessibility, audit the product before launch for conformance with accessibility guidelines that are referenced in any legislation and legal cases in the territories the product will be available in. At time of writing, this is usually WCAG 2.0 AA, but this has already changed to WCAG 2.1 AA for public services in Europe, so check the latest local guidance.

To gain the greatest legal protection, ensure the audit is done by an independent (usually external) expert who understands the referenced guidelines, and ideally has not worked on the product up to this point.

The cost of such testing depends on:

- The number of web pages or app screens in the product that the expert audits – use the recent WCAG-EM Website Accessibility Conformance Evaluation Methodology[13] to advise you on how to choose this in a justifiable way

- The number of accessibility issues (fails) found – the time needed to write an audit report documenting one fail could be a few hours; if sixty fails have been found, this can take more than a week

Ideally, an audit will be an expert rubber-stamping exercise because you have embedded accessibility testing internally to find and fix simple issues via cheaper and less expert mechanisms throughout design and development. If you have done this embedded testing, let your audit supplier know when you commission the audit as they may give you a discount from their usual rates.

Consider fixing any aspects of the product that fail to meet success criteria, or provide justification for why the required fixes are not reasonable to achieve – at all, or before launch – due to other project constraints. Audit reports that include cost-benefits analyses – for example, in the form of an Accessibility Issue Prioritisation Matrix (see later in this activity for more details) – will help you to do this in a justifiable way.

WCAG audits will give you a relatively cheap idea of how accessible your product may be to your target audiences in comparison to user testing, but they are not as reliable. They can tell you how well you've followed the specification, but can't tell you how usable your product will be for people with disabilities. For that you'll need to consider 'test-drive' tests.

'Test-drive' tests – testing user journeys with users and experts

Unlike the previous methodologies which test individual pages or screens against heuristics, 'test-drive' tests are based on user tasks.

Task-based testing checks that the product's target users can complete *all* the tasks that they come to the product to achieve, using their assistive technology or browser/OS accessibility settings, with reasonable efficiency and without any external prompting or help. As this models the actual user journeys and interactions that people will experience in your digital product, task-based testing is a more reliable methodology for proving that disabled people can use your product than heuristic testing.

To use a road-trip analogy, if heuristic testing checks to make sure you have made all the right turns according to the map to get where you wish to go, user testing encourages you to look out of the car window to see if you've ended up where you wished to be. While it may be more costly than 'checking the map', it is more reliable because it doesn't rely on the quality of the route in predicting where you *should* end up. It looks directly to see if you've actually *arrived*.

Pre-launch task-based user testing

The ideal type of task-based testing is done with real users. When you user-test a product with real people with disabilities, there is no simulation, no 'putting yourself in someone else's shoes'; you are working directly with the people who care most about the accessibility of your product, and they will tell you exactly whether they can achieve what they wished to achieve. And if not, where the blocks were.

If you are testing solely with disabled people, it may be unclear whether these blocks are to do with 'accessibility' or 'usability', so it's useful to include disabled and older people alongside users with no disabilities in your participants list for task-based user testing.

Which user groups to include

Consider including representatives of the following groups of disabled and older users in your user testing:

- Assistive technology users:

  - A blind screen reader user; a vision-impaired screen magnifier user; a low-vision user who uses resized text

  - A motor-impaired voice-activation user; a motor-impaired switch user

- Non-assistive technology users:

  - A user who is hard of hearing, deafened or deaf

  - A dyslexic user; a user with attention deficit hyperactivity disorder (ADHD) or Asperger's syndrome; a user with a moderate or severe learning difficulty

  - An older user (over the age of seventy-five)

This is a default list which you can modify based on your research in Activity 1 on which disabled user groups are more or less likely to be in the target audiences for your digital product.

You should be able to justify the number of participants that you test with in each user group (the sample size). Ideally, include at least a mix of beginners and experienced ICT system/assistive technology users in each group. For efficiency, much of the difference in user experience that disabled people might experience using different types of assistive technologies on one particular device or OS is best tested for separately via pre-launch assistive technology difference testing (see below). But as there are significant differences in the way assistive technologies function on different devices and OSes, ensure that you user-test the versions of the product you've created for each of the devices and OSes you will support with one of the assistive technologies you support on each device.

At Hassell Inclusion, we have been user testing products with people with and without disabilities for years. We've consistently refined our ways of working ever since I found that integrating people with disabilities into rounds of user testing with people without disabilities could save up to 40% of the costs of doing each separately. For inspiration on how to do this, see my SlideShare on 'Models for bringing accessibility and usability together'.[14]

At what points in the creation of a site or app can you include disabled and older people in user testing?

It is challenging to include assistive technology users in task-based user testing of websites or mobile apps in early stages of development, and the costs of including all groups in all rounds of user testing may be unreasonable, so I recommend you concentrate

on non-assistive technology users at earlier stages
of development, and include assistive technology
users when the product is mature enough for them
to meaningfully test.

This is what Judith Fellowes, an expert user
researcher who worked with me at the BBC, had to
say when I interviewed her:

> 'There are lots of access needs that you
> can easily incorporate into all rounds of
> testing. Where you sometimes might have
> more difficulty in testing the early stages of
> development (where you often test through
> paper prototyping, or where you've just got
> a couple of clickable images) is if you have
> got somebody who is using an assistive
> technology which is dependent on having
> a properly coded interface. But you can
> certainly accommodate these users, with a bit
> of effort.

> 'For example, in most user tests you might
> start off with a context interview to get
> background on people: how they like
> to engage and what they like to do. If
> you're including screen-reader users or
> magnification users, you may not be able to
> get them to have a look at your prototype, but

you could start understanding more about how they might want to operate, or how they do operate, digital products.

'What also works well is getting people to look at competitor sites so you can learn from access technology users' opinion of them. Then you can build up a pattern of how people would like things to work. There are a lot of different access needs that you could cover and you're obviously not going to be able to cover them in all rounds of testing, so you might want to include people who use assistive technologies at later stages.'

'Test-drive' tests – remote user testing, cognitive walkthroughs and exclusion audits

If you do not have the time or budget to do lab-based user testing of your product with disabled people, there are a couple of less effective but cheaper alternatives:

- Do *remote user testing* – testing conducted online – which can get you direct feedback from users in a 'quick and dirty' guerrilla-style[15]

- Engage the services of an expert who understands how disabled people use websites and mobile apps to conduct a *cognitive walkthrough*[16] – to go through your product's core user journeys, one step at a time, *as if* they were a person from each of the disabled and older user groups, noting down any issues or barriers that they consider would hinder that person's progress through the task

One interesting example of a cognitive walkthrough is the *exclusion audit* methodology, promoted in the EDC Inclusive Design Toolkit,[17] which is often used to assess the inclusiveness of non-digital products. My team has had some success using it with digital product teams with little experience of accessibility. We introduce team members to a set of personas of disabled people, ask each team member to put themselves in the shoes of one of the personas, work with them to break down the core user goals of the product into steps and assess what barriers a disabled person would find at each of those steps. In a couple of hours, this thought experiment gives team members a virtual experience of using the product as if they were one of its disabled users.

While the accuracy of the results of this exercise isn't sufficient to prove the accessibility of a product, exclusion audits can be a low-cost, highly engaging way of getting team members bought in to considering the accessibility of their product throughout its creation.

When you're doing exclusion audits for digital products, make sure you support the team to understand the added complexity of the technologies that lie between the product they're creating and the user experience their disabled users may get. With a non-digital design, in most cases, what you see is what you get. For digital products, the testers need to understand the accessibility ecosystem (see Activity 2) to correctly identify barriers to disabled people's use of the product with any degree of accuracy.

This is one of the reasons why I recommend that exclusion audits are best used for *educating* team members. You can only rely on the results if the cognitive walkthrough is done by a person who really understands disabled users' needs and the technologies they use to support those needs.

'Test-drive' tests – pre-launch browser and assistive technology difference testing

One final accessibility testing methodology to include in your pre-launch plan is testing of the product against all the supported browsers and assistive technologies you specified in Activity 3. This needs to be done by an expert that understands any differences that users would experience in viewing your product across those browsers and assistive technologies.

For example, the accessibility experience of newer HTML 5 elements can vary massively across different browsers and assistive technologies – see Graham Armfield's popular blogs on Native Element Accessibility.[18]

I recommend your team members do *not* test with any assistive technologies (especially screen readers like JAWS), unless they are trained in how disabled people who rely on them for access use them, to avoid false positives and true negatives due to inexperience. If you are not a screen reader user but you do need to test a page with one, I recommend using the combination of the Firefox browser and the free NVDA screen reader, and following the guidance in Marco Zehe's useful blog 'How to use NVDA and Firefox to test your web pages for accessibility'.[19]

Screen readers are the main assistive technology that may deliver (sometimes massive) differences in the quality of accessibility experience of a website or app across different brands and versions. So it makes sense to test your product with all the screen readers you chose to support to check that the user-testing results that you found with blind people using one screen reader can be reliably extrapolated to other types of screen reader. The creation of Voice Control for Mac and iOS and Voice Access for Android suggests it may also be sensible to test your product with the speech recognition systems available on each of the devices you support.

This assistive technology difference testing is similar in many ways to browser testing – ensuring that a good accessibility experience is available to all your audiences no matter which of the combinations of browsers and assistive technologies you specified in Activity 3 they are using. This is particularly necessary if your digital product involves any new or cutting-edge technologies (for example, dynamic/ rich internet experiences made accessible through WAI-ARIA) that may be supported by different browsers and assistive technologies in different ways.

Where you find issues during such testing that are due to differences in accessibility experience found between different combinations of browsers and assistive technologies, it is important to make a justifiable decision about whether to provide workarounds for a consistently good accessibility experience across all the combinations.

Choosing the right methodologies for your product, budget and deadlines

At the start of development, the project manager, or test manager if you have one, in conjunction with the rest of the team, should discuss and agree where accessibility will be tested in the project's test plan using any or all of the methodologies outlined above.

Your plan needs to assure you that you are directing the design and development of the product towards the level of accessibility experience that you are aiming for. Different project budgets will allow teams to do more or fewer rounds of testing, and choose more or less reliable indicators that the product will really deliver that level of accessibility experience.

Ensuring test schedules can flex

If planning for how you will assure the product's accessibility alongside its usability, security, resilience and browser/device independence is essential right from the start, then *sticking to the plan* during development is equally important.

One key thing here is the cost of postponing different kinds of testing if the product isn't ready on time.

My experience, from managing the BBC's resource of user testing specialists, is that the ability to accurately estimate the time it will take to develop a product is a rare quality in project teams. Invariably products are not delivered for testing on time, so a user testing specialist must strive to be flexible about the nature of testing they have scheduled.

As it can be expensive to reschedule test participants and test lab bookings, development and user testing teams need to keep in good communication during development. This is to ensure that the value the team wish to get from user testing is realised, even if they deliver the prototype an hour before testing is scheduled to begin.

Include time for fixes in your project planning

Your development schedule also needs to include time to *fix* the accessibility problems found in your testing. This seems an obvious point to make, but my team's experience is that where accessibility is not a priority for an organisation or project team, testing may have been scheduled, but without time being put aside for *fixing* accessibility issues that the testing uncovers.

The Accessibility Issue Prioritisation Matrix

Whatever testing methodology you use, it is essential to enable the product team to quickly assess any accessibility issues (defects) it finds and prioritise fixes on a cost-benefits basis. Therefore, test results should be reported in two standard ways that enable:

- Project management staff to quickly get a *strategic overview* of the number of issues and their relative importance, based on an analysis of the benefits of fixing each issue to the different disabled audiences it affects, and an estimate of the cost of implementing its proposed fix

- Implementation staff to understand each issue and its impact in *more detail* and apply the suggested fix

My team's experience of reading countless accessibility test reports is that the second of these – the technical information to help the people who'll actually fix issues – is usually well covered, but the essential overview information to enable the results of testing to be quickly and strategically understood and resources prioritised for fixing is often poorly done or completely missing. This then requires time-poor project management staff to read through hundreds of pages of detail to work out what the test results mean for their project planning.

To rectify this, I created the Accessibility Issue Prioritisation Matrix. This provides a way for testers to communicate the cost-benefits of fixing each issue found to product and project managers, to facilitate their discussion of prioritisation of fixes with all stakeholders.

The Accessibility Issue Prioritisation Matrix is a spreadsheet that provides an overview of all issues found in testing, with each line describing an issue, a unique reference number so it can be easily and precisely referred to in discussions, the suggested solution for fixing it and values for each of the four key factors that are most useful in prioritising fixes.

The four key factors are:

1. The *extent/frequency of occurrence* of the issue and the importance of the parts of the product in which the issue occurs:

   – Whether the issue occurs in an element which appears on every page across the whole site or app; on a section navigation page; or on a leaf page

INCLUSIVE DESIGN FOR PRODUCTS

- Whether the page(s) the element occurs on are part of the product's core user journeys or not

- How frequently the issue occurs

2. The *size of the audiences* that would experience difficulty in using the product because of the issue

3. The *impact* of the issue on their use of the product:

   - High = a total block to them completing a user journey

   - Medium = they can complete the user journey, but the issue will slow them down

   - Low = the issue is unlikely to impact them, in practice

4. The estimated *cost of fixing* the issue

The Accessibility Issue Prioritisation Matrix also includes three different cost-benefits measures for fixing the issue, calculated from the four key factors using business intelligence embedded in the spreadsheet:

1. *Value for money* – the number of people affected by the issue, multiplied by the impact of how much it affects them (the benefits) vs the estimated costs of fixing it

2. *Political risk aversion* – the political weight (in terms of adverse PR and litigiousness) of the disabled groups affected by the issue, multiplied by the impact of how much it affects them (the benefits) vs the estimated costs of fixing it

3. A *blend of these two measures*

Choose one of these cost-benefits measures to use based on your organisation's motivation for accessibility (for how to set this, see Chapter 4 of this book's companion, *Inclusive Design for Organisations*).

You can then use the spreadsheet's reordering function to place the issues in the prioritisation order that corresponds to your organisation's values and work through them from the most important to the least important, deciding which fixes you can budget for and which you cannot.

The Accessibility Issue Prioritisation Matrix has been so universally useful for Hassell Inclusion clients that I have included a version of it for free in the support materials for this book. I would recommend that you review it, together with its documentation and case study, to see whether it would help you to quickly understand and action the prioritisation of accessibility fixes in your project process. If you need further help or training in using it, contact us at Hassell Inclusion.[20]

How to reduce the cost of fixes where you cannot easily change the code

If testing finds that there are accessibility issues with websites or components that you have procured, and you don't have the ability or competence to make code fixes, then *accessibility remediation tools*, such as Deque's Amaze,[21] could be a way of fixing the issues. These tools create server-side overlays that fix accessibility bugs by replacing deficient code with stored layers of accessible code, but I do not recommend them for products that you are able to fix in more established ways. They often cost more over time than doing fixes yourself, do not increase your team's ability to deliver accessible products and the overlays can often break with site maintenance.[22]

What to do when you can't please everyone

If the results of your testing indicate that the design, code or content of your evolving product is working for most users but not for some disabled users, then ideally you will be able to find cost-effective ways of fixing your product to work for those disabled users without negatively impacting the user experience of your non-disabled users. But sometimes this isn't possible.

A fix that improves the user experience of one disabled user group may damage the user experience of another disabled user group, or the larger number of people with no disability or impairment. In this case – where your testing finds that the ideal of inclusive design isn't possible for your product – the user-personalised approaches we discussed in Activity 5 are a possible way of getting around these difficulties, if you have the time and money to include them.

NOW IT'S YOUR TURN

- Use the web accessibility development planning template to guide you in holding a workshop to plan accessibility testing across the length of your product's development

- To inspire you, here's a summary of an accessibility testing plan for a homepage with new personalisation functionality we worked on years ago:

  - Initial testing of prototype wireframes of the page with non-disabled people to check their reaction to the idea of being able to rearrange the sections of the page

  - WCAG checkpoint testing for each *element* of the functionality of the homepage as it is developed

- Iterative user testing with disabled and non-disabled people of the *complete* homepage at the end of every sprint

- Once that user testing proves a great user experience, do follow-up testing of the page against various different types of screen reader to check that the user testing results can be extrapolated reliably to the other supported screen readers

c. Making decisions about launch from an accessibility point of view

By this point you'll have been developing your product for quite some while, and hopefully your iterative testing is finding that most people are not only interested in using it, but they also find it a usable experience. Often the problem is that the product doesn't yet deliver that usable experience to everyone. So the issue is: how good does its accessibility need to be for it to be ready to launch?

That's the key decision behind this final part of Activity 6: does your product's accessibility need to be perfect? And if you do decide to launch without perfect accessibility, what are the implications of that?

How good does the accessibility in a 'version 1' product have to be?

The important thing to bear in mind here is that no product is launched which is bug-free. Launch planning is not about perfect products at some vague point in the future, but about having a product that is good enough for launch now.

The trick here may be to act like Google, Facebook, Amazon, Twitter and many other successful websites: ship early, and then improve your product over time. Check out the version 1 of these and many other websites at 'What the World's Biggest Websites Looked Like at Launch'.[23] I guarantee that you'll be amazed at what is missing from the sites.

The thing that makes these giants household names, rather than the hundreds of competitors who failed to win that success, is the question of when to ship. How good does your digital product have to be?

That comes down to what's important – what you reckon is the minimum level of quality and functionality for your product to be useful to users and make the right sort of mark against your competitors (assuming you have some). If your product demonstrates enough of its USPs and no more than that, you've achieved your minimal viable product, so get it out there right now.

If you're too early, your target audiences may consider it a false start and not bother coming back in the future; too late, and they may have found what they were looking for somewhere else, so you'll have to spend half your time working out how to get them to switch to you. The important thing here is that while it's you making the judgement of whether you're ready to go, it's your target audiences that will decide whether you got it right. They are the people who will make your product successful or not.

This is the reality of modern digital product development: products evolve quickly through numerous minor and fewer major versions, whether explicitly via updates through an app store or, less transparently, as tweaks to a website. All features in a product's backlog are constantly being assigned and reassigned to different product versions. So most product managers wouldn't consider it unreasonable to expect accessibility functionality to follow suit.

You will need to consider how good the accessibility of your product has to be in the definition of your minimal viable product, which depends on how important the disabled groups in your target audiences will be to its success.

For most digital products that my team has been involved with, the minimal viable product has allowed for launch with some accessibility quality deficiencies, or missing accessibility features, as long as the accessibility risk in making this decision is deemed acceptable by the organisation's lawyers. Organisations make a call on which compromises they're willing to launch with and which they are not. The only exceptions to this that I've experienced are:

- Where the product's target audiences are primarily made up of disabled people

- Where it will not be possible to sell the product in key territories unless it meets a defined accessibility threshold – for example, Section 508 in the USA, EN 301 549 in Europe, and selling products into Australia since the 2013 DDA came into force

- If some accessibility advocates get their way and Apple and Google require an app to be accessible for them to include it in their app stores[24]

If you do decide to launch without full accessibility, as I believe is inevitable on all but the simplest digital product development:

- The decision to launch version 1 with accessibility deficiencies needs to be justifiable

- The delivery of missing accessibility features or accessibility quality needs to be planned for in subsequent versions

- Communicate the deficiencies and timetable for fixing them to disabled users via an *accessibility statement* to allow you to manage audience expectations (see next activity)

At a more granular level, the accessibility of each new item of content on your website may be subject to the same decisions about whether to post now or wait for full accessibility quality.

To give an example: if you are live streaming video of an important news event on your website but do not have the ability to provide captions or a transcript in real time, should you delay publishing that stream until you do? Or should you publish the stream and place a note next to it saying that captions and transcripts will be available in one day, and if users have any difficulties with that delay, they can contact you on your organisation's accessibility email address? Obviously, it would be better to have the full accessible solution available at the time of the news event so there is full equality of access. But where that is not possible, how many people would actually be helped by holding back the stream until captions and a transcript were available?

This consideration is particularly important for news organisations as one of the main purposes of their websites and mobile apps is likely to be 'to report news items as soon as possible'. This purpose may even be a USP of the organisation against their competitors (to always be first with the story, rather than best at telling the story). Where this is the case, the cost to the organisation of holding back news coverage for accessibility or any other reason may be too much to accept. And this may be the basis for their justification of publishing all news immediately and then enriching it with accessibility cues later in the day (see my blog: 'GLAD vs CNN closed-captions lawsuit: finding a win-win for broadcasters and deaf people'[25]).

Handling trade-offs between accessibility and other values of the product

Discussions of these trade-offs between accessibility and the product's other values (such as being first to break a story) cannot be found in any technical accessibility guidelines. They are designed to cover general situations and be applied to any website or app. But that doesn't make careful consideration of these trade-offs any less valid and important.

This is the reason why I believe that conformance with accessibility guidelines should always be balanced with safeguarding imperatives arising from the purpose of the product and its target audiences – no organisation can afford guidelines to dictate conformance if that conformance undermines its product's delivery on its purpose. Handling these real-world trade-offs is the job of the product manager and the team maintaining the product. And ISO 30071-1 allows them the flexibility to include these imperatives when they are making decisions about accessibility, just as long as they communicate their decisions to users who may be adversely affected.

So how should you make decisions about any accessibility compromises you are considering for a particular product or product-version launch? In essence, the decision is quite simple:

- Do the *benefits* of being able to launch your product or product version right now (for example, to meet deadlines dictated by an advertising campaign or launch event for the product) outweigh the potential *risks* of releasing the product with accessibility deficiencies?

- Is there a way of *mitigating those risks* by communicating clearly and transparently with the audiences the accessibility deficiencies may impact?

ISO 30071-1 advises that the best way of mitigating these risks is to provide an accessibility statement, which is the subject of the next activity.

NOW IT'S YOUR TURN

If you are nearing the launch date for your product and still have remaining accessibility issues that testing has found, but which you know you will not have time to fix before launch, use the Accessibility Issue Prioritisation Matrix in this book's support materials to assess the resulting accessibility risk.

ACTIVITY 7

Ensure Communication About Accessibility

At this point, it's likely that you've just decided to launch your digital product without its accessibility being absolutely perfect, so how can ensuring two-way communications with your disabled users about the accessibility of your product help you mitigate the risk in doing that, and even help you minimise the cost of user testing going forwards?

The document that can help you achieve this is your product's *ICT system accessibility statement*, and Activity 7 is all about how to write it.

a. Creating your accessibility statement

Accessibility statements have been around for a
long while; certainly since the forerunner to BS 8878,
PAS-78, was launched in 2006. Unfortunately, many
organisations use them in misguided PR attempts to
let disabled people know how much work they've
done to make their websites accessible.

Reading most accessibility statements, you would be
forgiven for thinking that the websites on which you
find them are paragons of virtue and best practice
when it comes to accessibility, but this is rarely the
case. Most accessibility statements generally come
over as 'protesting too much', especially where
disabled users' experience of the website quickly
tells them that the organisation does not care about
accessibility in the way that its statement portrays.
Even recent requirements for accessibility statements
in the UK Public Sector Bodies (Websites and Mobile
Applications) (No 2) Accessibility Regulations 2018[1]
start well, but then fall into the trap of mandating
the presentation of lots of technical accessibility
information.

This misses the point. Accessibility statements
are tools of *expectation management*. And disabled

people's expectations of a digital product's accessibility may differ across different types of product.

As websites, and legislation requiring their accessibility, have existed for a long time, disabled people expect websites to be accessible. So it is likely that the only reason people will visit a website's accessibility statement is because something on the site is not working for them and they're looking for an explanation. In this situation, the purpose of the statement is to defuse their frustration. So basing your accessibility statement around explanations for any *deficiencies* of your product, rather than providing bland statements of conformance with guidelines, makes it much more likely to be useful for disabled people and for upholding your brand reputation. To be effective, the statement needs to be easily found from any page the user visits (for example, through a navigational link).

For apps, disabled people's expectations may be different. The link between the accessibility of mobile apps and existing legislation is still being clarified in many countries. And while I have seen lawsuits about the accessibility of EFTPOS terminals and airport kiosks, I've never seen any about apps for wearable devices, games or AR. People with disabilities are used to working out which apps have been designed to be accessible and which have not, so providing information on the accessibility that you *have* been able to provide in your app in your accessibility statement on your website, and putting a link to it in the app's App Store/Google Play documentation, may be exactly what disabled people are looking for.

How to write an effective accessibility statement

With these insights in mind, ISO 30071-1 recommends that accessibility statements:

- Use clear, simple language that the greatest majority of disabled users (including those with learning difficulties) can understand (even if they cannot so easily understand the rest of the site).

- Include information on how disabled users can customise their experience of the product if they are having difficulties using it – either through installing assistive technologies, using browser or OS accessibility preferences (for example linking to BBC My Web My Way[2] or WAI's Tips for Customizing your Computer[3]), or via user-personalisation/individualisation tools in the product itself.

- Include information on any accessibility deficiencies the product has, any plans to fix those deficiencies, and any alternative accessible means which have been provided to help affected users get around these deficiencies in the meantime.

- Include an accessible contact mechanism for disabled people to use to get help if they still can't find a solution to their difficulties. ISO 30071-1 recommends that the statement suggests users read WAI's 'Contacting Organizations about Inaccessible Websites'[4] document to make sure their feedback adequately explains the difficulty they are having, so the product team can more easily understand and reproduce it.

After this information, the statement *may* include information on how the owners of the product have catered for accessibility in its development. While this may include references to standards and guidelines and the product's level of conformance with them, it should avoid technical terms and jargon.

Finally, the accessibility statement should include the date it was last updated, so that users can see it is a live document whose accuracy is reviewed and updated every time a new version of the product is released.

What is the value of accessibility conformance badges?

Many accessibility statements include conformance badges from suppliers who audited the product. These aim to help organisations feel more secure about accessibility at launch, but while the costs of badges are clear, the benefits are harder to assess.

If you are considering paying for a badge to add to your accessibility statement, consider:

- Its value to *you*, the product owner, in providing some sort of external independent proof and public recognition that your product has achieved a particular level of accessibility. Badges from different organisations use different metrics, so when you're choosing an organisation to audit and accredit your site, ask for details on how its badge is going to give you the level of accessibility assurance that you desire (and are willing to pay for).

- Its value to *your disabled users* in giving them information on whether the site will support their particular needs. Many badges do not do this well, so when you're choosing an organisation to audit and accredit your site, ask what mechanisms it will provide to ensure people with disabilities understand what the badge means and how it will allow them to predict whether the product will work for their particular needs.

You can get further information on the benefits and limitations of accessibility conformance badges from my popular blog: '5 things you should know before buying accessibility audit and accreditation services'.[5]

b. What can happen if you get your communication wrong

It's worth noting that the costs to your organisation of neglecting to communicate issues that will affect your disabled users' accessibility experience of your product, or doing your communication poorly, can be more significant than you may expect. Here are a few examples from my team's experience:

- Providing an insufficiently clear explanation of justifiable reasoning for not providing a completely accessible version of every iPlayer feature resulted in me having to spend a lot of costly time defending the product's accessibility on BBC radio and TV (see my story in Chapter 1), despite the product winning multiple awards for accessibility[6]

- Not giving disabled users a simple way of feeding back their concerns about a product's accessibility is likely to raise their existing frustration, and may potentially be a factor in them contacting the product owner through a legal proxy rather than directly

- Omitting to include instructions to guide disabled users in making feedback effective can result in time-consuming chains of phone or email correspondence between the users and the product's customer-service team

Here's an example from Jennison Asuncion, Engineering Manager for Accessibility at LinkedIn, and previously IT Accessibility Consultant at Royal Bank of Canada, in my interview with him:

'Many companies now have information on accessible features that they have for their business, whether it's a restaurant or whatnot in Ontario. I'm not going to claim to be an expert about the AODA, but what I will say is that part of what the act obligates businesses to do is to provide information on how their services are accessible.

'What I've seen is people will put that stuff up on their website and they'll say, "Here's information on our accessibility plan." Well I, Jennison, who's blind, will download what I think is going to be a useful file. I open it up and it's an inaccessible untagged PDF. So I shake my head and go, "What's the point?"'

NOW IT'S YOUR TURN

- Create an accessibility statement for your product based on the advice in this chapter and my popular blog: 'How to write an effective Accessibility Statement'[7]; make sure you include documentation of any deficiencies in the version of the product that you are readying for launch

- You can use the accessibility statement on hassellinclusion.com[8] as an example of best practice

ACTIVITY 8

Ensure Integration Of Accessibility In System Updates

'We've created this product to be accessible. It's up to you now to make sure you don't screw that up.'

That was the first line a client asked me to include in an accessibility maintenance manual that I created for them. And the tone is justified. After all the hard work they'd done to make things accessible for launch, sloppy decisions made by content staff, who could easily have got them right, could leave the product's accessibility victory vulnerable to death by a thousand cuts.

In a product's history, more time elapses after launch than before it, and much of its content is created after launch. This activity is essential to ensure a great start with accessibility doesn't get ruined. Or conversely, that a poor start gets remedied before too much reputational damage is done.

Activity 8 is all about planning to maintain or even improve accessibility in all post-launch versions and maintenance. There are two types of activities here:

- *Proactive activities* that you initiate to freshen or improve your product

- *Reactive activities* that are forced on you by changes in the browsers, devices or contexts in which your audiences use your product

a. Proactive activity: upholding accessibility during minor product maintenance

Let's start with ensuring that the digital product's accessibility doesn't degrade through its maintenance. This can be a challenge, because often the people in charge of *maintaining* a product are not the same people who were in charge of *creating* it.

As well as content updates, the performance of many digital products often gets iterated through post-launch optimisation routines to test how small changes to components of the product's UI may impact how successful the product is. On retail websites, for example, A-B testing focuses on which interface options maximise conversion through any sales funnels. But optimisations can make accessibility worse as they improve performance. SEO optimisation can require all images on a site to have alt-text so they can be found in image searches, but this can result in alt-text being added to images which shouldn't have it because they are purely decorative.

You therefore need to transfer all of the awareness of the need for accessibility, and how to achieve it, from the product creation team to its maintenance teams. This is challenging, especially as it may often be the case that the number of people maintaining content on a website or mobile app is many times higher than the number of people on the team that created it. Moreover, for organisations that create versions of their products for different territories, one set of site or app page templates could be localised, tweaked and reused by many content teams spread all over the world.

You have three options for helping your maintenance team to get things right:

1. Assume that they will get things wrong unless you spend money putting in place continuous accessibility auditing tools to *police bad practice*

2. Spend money training your maintenance team members in content accessibility, embedding motivation and best practice so they *want to get things right* and *are able to do so*

3. Spend money embedding best practice in the CMS the team members will use to maintain and create content, so they *can't get things wrong.*

As the third of these is the most scalable solution, let's start with understanding that.

Embedding accessibility support within your CMS

Chances are, your project will have delivered a CMS to maintain the product's content, as well as the product itself. This CMS will ideally embed best practice by preventing authors from adversely affecting the accessibility coding of page templates by mistake and requiring them to create accessible content. The best standards after all are not ones that you have to read, but ones that are embedded in tools to such an extent that you cannot help but follow them.

So it is with authoring tools and CMSs – the best way of ensuring a digital product's continued high level of accessibility is to make sure its CMS automates, requires and facilitates various accessibility cues to be included by content authors.

For example, the CMS can:

- *Automatically* mark-up text formatting (like heading, bullets, bold and italics) entered into its rich-text editor with the correct semantics

- *Require* authors to include alt-text with images, or else the 'add image' widget won't allow the image to be included on a page

- *Facilitate* the creation of captions for video by providing links to tools that content authors can use to create them efficiently – for example, embedding access to YouTube's ability to automatically create captions from transcripts[1] or Amara's workflows that help you commission people anywhere in the world to create the captions for you cheaply[2]

W3C's ATAG[3] is a great resource to help you create the specification your CMS needs to have to facilitate content accessibility before and after launch. With the right CMS in place, content staff only need to be trained in how to create and publish content in a way that makes use of all of its accessibility settings and features.

Embedding accessibility within your content authoring teams

If you are not planning to deliver a CMS as part of the back end of your digital product, provide specific accessibility guidelines and training for content authors maintaining the site so they understand their responsibility easily, without needing to wade through guidance directed at development staff.

Also train your content authors in the justifiable reasoning practices that you've applied while developing the digital product. These will help them deal with situations when it may not be possible or reasonable to ensure that each piece of new or edited content is accessible to everyone. See the 'captioning of live streaming' example in Activity 6, and what Brian Kelly, Director of UK Web Focus, said when I interviewed him:

'When WCAG were first produced in 1997, we had a view that web resources were just being created by small groups of people. Back then, the web was a scarce resource, and effort could be put into ensuring that all resources created conformed to particular guidelines.

'Now, there are millions of resources being created every day by huge numbers of people. So the requirement which says every individual resource must conform to a particular set of guidelines may not be a scalable solution. There's the need to acknowledge the things that we can do and the things that we can't do. Things that are appropriate and things that aren't appropriate.

'With my mobile phone, every day I'm curating digital resources. I'm taking a photo, I'm uploading it to Instagram or Flickr, I'm tweeting it. Some of these times I don't think about the accessibility, because it's not really relevant. But when I'm writing a blog post, I have a large audience, so I do provide alt-text on my images.

'Or you may get your laptop out and write a paper and it's published. In our sphere, that's likely to be available on the web. So should you have ensured the Word or PDF resource conforms with accessibility guidelines?

'There's decision making that we are going through, or should be going through, each day. BS 8878 (and ISO 30071-1) have value because they make those decisions concrete.'

Embedding continuous accessibility testing tools

The types of accessibility error that may be made before launch and in post-launch maintenance are quite different:

- Accessibility errors *before* launch are invariably to do with the architectural design and coding of page templates, including navigation, branding and interactive elements like forms and transactional workflows

- Accessibility errors in *post-launch maintenance* are invariably to do with the accessibility of content, such as images, videos or text

The types of testing that are effective differ too:

- *Before launch*, task-based user testing of key pages, page elements and user journeys is the most reliable form of testing to ensure disabled people can use your product.

- *After launch,* accessibility errors introduced through content maintenance – an image missing alt-text or an article missing headings – are likely to be less severe, more localised in impact and more distributed across the content of the site. For this reason, automated accessibility testing, especially for large websites with hundreds of people creating content, can be very useful. This should be able to identify where any errors have been introduced on a day-by-day basis, highlighting these errors to the product owner in a high-level dashboard view and automatically generating requests for content owners to fix accessibility errors in the content they have created.

b. Proactive activity: upholding accessibility when making new releases of the product

New versions of digital products are released to add new functionality, restructure creaking information hierarchies, respond to changes in the context in which the product is used or just to keep it 'fresh'.

When I was at the BBC, most websites were refreshed with a major new version every eighteen months. In contrast, new releases of many mobile apps are made every month.

Always aim for accessibility quality to be upheld or improved when you are creating new versions of a digital product. Each release should ensure that any accessibility deficiencies that were identified but not fixed in the previous version are addressed. This will help keep your disabled and older users loyal to your product. But if you don't carefully consider the frequency of these updates, it is possible, if you're not careful, that changing the product too often could lose you as many users as it attracts.

One of the qualities that marks out an experienced product manager is how they plan for and handle large product updates. While product updates always aim to deliver a better product than the previous version, whenever you change a product in any big way, there will be a period in which your users may feel uncomfortable as they have to *relearn* how to use your product. You may recall my example of this from BBC iPlayer in Chapter 1.

It is not uncommon for the number of people using your product immediately after an update to go through a dip, as existing users decide whether to go to the bother of relearning how to use it, and the new users that your redesign aims to reach have yet to establish a relationship with your product that makes them return to it day by day.

I mention this here because, while these new version 'audience dips' are common for all digital products, they are most marked for disabled and older people who find learning and *relearning* how to use websites and apps more of a challenge. This 'relearning inertia' is normally useful for product owners – if your product can attract disabled users and they can learn how to use it, they are much less likely than other users to switch to a competitor's product on a whim. On the other hand, when you launch a new version of your product, it may be as easy for them to learn to use the competitor's product as it is to relearn your new version.

To retain your users' loyalty, you need to make sure that you *actively* support all of your users, especially disabled and older users, in easily relearning how to use your new product. Do this by providing guidance for how they can do what they used to do in the old version and any new things that they can now do that they couldn't before. You also need to make sure you don't change the page structure or navigation of your site or app too often, as changes that might be obvious for non-disabled users who are confident in the use of technology may not be as easy to handle for disabled and older users.

As Jennison Asuncion, Engineering Manager for Accessibility at LinkedIn, said when I interviewed him:

> 'There was a survey or some research done that showed that for people with disabilities, change is something they have challenge with. Blind and low-vision folks in particular can have trouble with site redesigns.

> 'Fully seeing people, if your website changes, can eyeball the entire screen quickly and see how everything is laid out, whereas a screen reader is linear. It's left to right, top to bottom. So if things have moved around, like if you've moved a link from the top left to the bottom right, for a sighted person, sure it might take you a second, but you'll see. But for the average blind person who's going to your site, it may take them a bit of time, or they might not even see that the new link is buried somewhere else on the site.

> 'It's almost like if you've rearranged a house. You've decided to move the coffee table to another part of the living room, for example.

When I walk in, I'm used to it being on the left-hand side. You as a sighted person are walking into the room and you see the coffee table has moved. I walk into the room, and if no one else is with me, I'll whack myself right into it. From then on, I'll know it's there, but it's one of those things I don't think people think about from that perspective.

'When you're totally blind like myself, you definitely notice. I'm not saying people can't change around their sites, because that's important; you want to keep things fresh. But maybe three months ahead of time, before those changes go into the website, you might start having little banners saying, "Coming soon, a new website, a new look and feel." Maybe blind users can click on or activate a link and maybe there's a video or some text there that says, "This is what we're planning to do."'

You can find out more about how to avoid losing loyal users by handling site updates well in my blog 'Relearnability – how to keep your disabled users through a website redesign.'[4]

Finally, when you make a major update, make sure that your product's ICT system accessibility log and statement are updated, detailing any existing accessibility deficiencies you've fixed and any deficiencies introduced in the new features. An out-of-date statement is rarely any use to anyone, which is why accessibility statements should include a 'last-updated' date.

c. Reactive activity: responding to changes in technology after launch

One thing that is often overlooked after launch is that the *context* in which your users use your product changes over time.

It is important to revisit the research in your ICT system accessibility log as time goes on to check that the findings are still true. In the same way that your product will go through versions, so will the assistive technologies that disabled people will access it through and the types of device they'll use it on.

While it is not always the case that disabled people keep up to date with the newest version of the assistive technology that they use (for example, they may not be able to afford to do so), it is worth keeping an eye on any new versions of the assistive technologies that you support because, like new browsers or OSes, they may potentially break the existing good user experience of your product because they use a new underlying technology or engine. Or they may simply just have bugs.

While none of these situations are the fault of the product manager, if enough of your users with disabilities upgrade to the new version and it doesn't work well with your product, then you may have to make a difficult decision – whether to divert team resources from delivering your product's roadmap of updates to re-establish the good user experience people used to have with the new assistive technology version.

While having to deal with such unplanned sources of work may be frustrating, they are a common factor of digital product development. Dealing with new assistive technology updates is not much more onerous than having to deal with new versions of browsers or OSes when they are released.

d. Reactive activity: responding to accessibility feedback

Finally, make sure that all audience feedback about the digital product's accessibility, which is likely to come through your organisation's accessibility email address (or some other communication channel specified in your product's accessibility statement), is consistently handled well.

As we at Hassell Inclusion often say to our clients, 'All feedback is a gift that might blow up in your face if you don't treat it correctly.' Each accessibility lawsuit probably started out with a complaint from a user about an accessibility deficiency of a digital product. If complaints are handled correctly from the start, it's likely that most potential legal threats can be avoided.

So how should you correctly deal with accessibility feedback from your users? Firstly, you need to check whether the feedback is a comment or a complaint.

If it's a comment, send a standardised response thanking the user for their feedback and keep the comment in your log, as it may just help you work out how to improve the product when you're planning the next version. If it is a complaint, you need to be able to get to the bottom of the issue as quickly and efficiently as possible. So it is essential to:

- Understand what the problem is

- Verify whether the problem has been caused by an accessibility deficiency in your digital product or is due to user error

This is why ISO 30071-1 suggests that sites include advice on how to make a complaint about accessibility in their accessibility statement via a link to WAI's 'Contacting Organizations about Inaccessible Websites' (see Activity 7). This document advises disabled people on the information they need to provide to website owners:

- What type of disability they have

- What assistive technology, browser and OS they are using

- What page or pages they experienced the problem on

- What exactly the problem is

- How serious they regard it to be

This information will give you a chance of understanding and replicating the problem the user is having, as long as your help centre and support staff know who on your maintenance team to pass the call to, and that person has some expertise in understanding how disabled people use digital and has the assistive technologies available that the person is using.

However, for most organisations it does not make sense to train maintenance staff to become experts in using assistive technologies just so that they can replicate and investigate accessibility problems users report concerning your digital product. You could invite the user to demonstrate their problem to you, either by them visiting your offices or you going to the place where they normally use your product. For those product teams that have not been able to afford to do user testing of the product with disabled people, such a demonstration can be a real eye opener and does not require the expense of recruiting or incentivising disabled people to take part in research.

The only potential negative in dealing with accessibility complaints in this personal way is if you cannot fix the problem because of some technical issue. But even in this case, with the right expectation management from the beginning, you are better placed to explain to the user the justifiable reasons why you cannot fix their problem and mitigate the accessibility risk caused by not being able to meet their needs.

NOW IT'S YOUR TURN

- Use the ICT system accessibility log template to guide you in planning for how you will maintain the accessibility of your product after launch

- Find a scalable way of getting accessibility training for all staff who maintain your digital products

What's Next?

I've aimed in this book to introduce you to the activities that can help embed accessibility and inclusive design into your digital production process, so you can create products that include more of your missing 20%.

I hope that you wish to join the increasing number of organisations, product owners and accessibility advocates who are working towards a future of more inclusive digital products.

I'd encourage you to resolve to become a master at implementing the activities, like some of the people I've interviewed for this book. Seek out opportunities to implement ISO 30071-1 across many different products (and organisations, if you're inclined towards consultancy). Seek out mentoring from people who have been there before you in how to deal with the specific challenges of each product and organisation. And keep up to date with accessibility thought leaders, as the nature of digital is that there's always something new happening, and accessibility is no different.

If you're interested in setting up a wider accessibility strategy for products in your organisation, then I encourage you to read this book's companion, *Inclusive Design for Organisations*. This will help you to ensure that accessibility isn't just something that's done well for your product, but it's done consistently well throughout your organisation.

Accessibility is a journey. Thanks for coming with me a few more steps along the path.

Here's to your next steps!

Get help for the rest of your journey from:

http://qrs.ly/3a4a6bm

And please get in touch if I can help you further.

Jonathan Hassell
www.hassellinclusion.com

References

Foreword

1   www.ncbi.nlm.nih.gov/pubmed/27044605
2   gapm.io/incm
3   www.un.org/development/desa/en/news/population/world
    -population-prospects-2019.html

Chapter 1

1   www.hassellinclusion.com/blog/rnib-bmi-baby-accessibility
    -lawsuit
2   http://en.wikipedia.org/wiki/Achilles'_heel
3   http://en.wikipedia.org/wiki/Sam_Farber

Chapter 2

1   https://neilpatel.com/what-is-growth-hacking
2   www.slideshare.net/jonathanhassell/case-studies-of-implementing
    -bs-8878-csun-2012-12145101/31
3   www.inclusivedesigntoolkit.com
4   www.iso.org/iso/catalogue_detail.htm?csnumber=52075
5   www.hassellinclusion.com/blog/effective-websites-bs-8878
    -website-in-1-day
6   Seminar no longer available online; interview with Neil at: https://
    calvium.com/interview-with-neil-collard-from-bristol-agency-e3
7   www.bbc.co.uk/blogs/bbcinternet/2011/04/making_the_right
    _products_in_t.html
8   www.rnib.org.uk/audio-description-on-BBC
9   www.insidehighered.com/news/2017/03/06/u-california-berkeley
    -delete-publicly-available-educational-content
10 http://en.wikipedia.org/wiki/Outliers_(book)
11 www.eeoc.gov/policy/docs/accommodation.html#general

Activity 1

1   www.paulgraham.com/startupideas.html
2   www.ons.gov.uk/peoplepopulationandcommunity
    /householdcharacteristics/homeinternetandsocialmediausage
    /bulletins/internetaccesshouseholdsandindividuals/2018
3   http://downloads.bbc.co.uk/mediacentre/iplayer/iplayer
    -performance-jan19.pdf
4   https://adwords.google.co.uk/KeywordPlanner
5   www.problogger.net/archives/2005/08/15/search-engine
    -optimization-for-blogs
6   www.worldometers.info/world-population/uk-population
7   www.gov.uk/government/statistics/family-resources-survey
    -financial-year-201617
8   www.ons.gov.uk/peoplepopulationandcommunity
    /populationandmigration/populationestimates/articles
    /overviewoftheukpopulation/november2018
9   https://fivethirtyeight.com/features/what-baby-boomers
    -retirement-means-for-the-u-s-economy
10 www.gov.uk/government/statistics/family-resources-survey
    -financial-year-201617
11 www.actiononhearingloss.org.uk/about-us/our-research-and
    -evidence/facts-and-figures
12 www.gov.uk/government/publications/understanding-disabilities
    -and-impairments-user-profiles/simone-dyslexic-user
13 https://assets.publishing.service.gov.uk/government/uploads
    /system/uploads/attachment_data/file/692771/family-resources
    -survey-2016-17.pdf
14 https://assets.publishing.service.gov.uk/government/uploads
    /system/uploads/attachment_data/file/692771/family-resources
    -survey-2016-17.pdf
15 https://assets.publishing.service.gov.uk/government/uploads
    /system/uploads/attachment_data/file/692771/family-resources
    -survey-2016-17.pdf
16 https://assets.publishing.service.gov.uk/government/uploads
    /system/uploads/attachment_data/file/692771/family-resources
    -survey-2016-17.pdf
17 www.nhs.uk/conditions/vision-loss
18 www.thecommunicationtrust.org.uk/media/2612/communication
    difficulties-_facts_and_stats.pdf
19 www.autism.org.uk/about/what-is/myths-facts-stats.aspx
20 www.mstrust.org.uk/a-z/prevalence-and-incidence-multiple
    -sclerosis
21 www.sportengland.org/media/3988/mapping-disability-the-facts
    .pdf

22 www.gov.uk/government/publications/sen-analysis-and-summary
-of-data-sources
23 www.sportengland.org/media/3988/mapping-disability-the-facts
.pdf
24 www.statista.com/statistics/281174/uk-population-by-age
25 www.ons.gov.uk/employmentandlabourmarket/peopleinwork
/employmentandemployeetypes/datasets/labourmarketstatusofdis
abledpeoplea08
26 www.scope.org.uk/campaigns/extra-costs
27 https://webarchive.nationalarchives.gov.uk/20121204131438/http://
www.culture.gov.uk/images/publications/maria-miller-speech
-launch-e-accessibility.pdf
28 www.ons.gov.uk/businessindustryandtrade/itandinternetindustry
/bulletins/internetusers/2018#older-adults-are-less-likely-to-use
-the-internet
29 www.ons.gov.uk/businessindustryandtrade/itandinternetindustry
/bulletins/internetusers/2018#older-adults-are-less-likely-to-use
-the-internet
30 https://adwords.google.co.uk/KeywordPlanner
31 http://calc.inclusivedesigntoolkit.com
32 https://itunes.apple.com/gb/app/bbc-cbeebies-playtime
/id684211403?mt=8
33 www.simplypsychology.org/maslow.html

Activity 2

1 www.w3.org/WAI/intro/people-use-web
2 www.bbc.co.uk/accessibility/best_practice/case_studies
3 http://webaim.org
4 http://webaim.org/projects/screenreadersurvey
5 https://accessibility.blog.gov.uk
6 https://accessibility.blog.gov.uk/2016/11/01/results-of-the-2016-gov
-uk-assistive-technology-survey
7 www.hassellinclusion.com/blog
8 www.hassellinclusion.com/topics/native-element-accessibility
9 https://en.wikipedia.org/wiki/Xbox_Adaptive_Controller
10 www.bbc.co.uk/accessibility/best_practice/case_studies
11 www.pewresearch.org/fact-tank/2017/04/07/disabled-americans
-are-less-likely-to-use-technology
12 https://hechingerreport.org/many-low-income-families-get-on-the
-internet-with-smartphones-or-tablets-that-matters-heres-why/
13 https://spacedoutandsmiling.com/presentations/autism-apple
-watch-independent-living-csun-2017

14 https://news.microsoft.com/2004/02/02/new-research-study-shows-57-percent-of-adult-computer-users-can-benefit-from-accessible-technology

15 www.techradar.com/uk/news/wwdc-2019-liveblog

16 www.linkedin.com/feed/update/urn:li:activity:6553157055975313408

17 https://gettecla.com/blogs/news/new-accessibility-features-to-ios-13-voice-control-more

18 www.hassellinclusion.com/blog/accessibility-developing-countries

19 https://techcrunch.com/2019/06/11/internet-trends-report-2019

20 www.digitaltrends.com/cars/what-is-apple-carplay

21 https://techcrunch.com/2019/06/11/internet-trends-report-2019

22 https://deviceatlas.com/blog/android-v-ios-market-share

23 https://webaim.org/projects/screenreadersurvey7/#mobileplatforms

24 http://takesugar.wordpress.com/2014/07/22/accessibility-head-to-head-android-vs-apple

25 http://recombu.com/digital/news/voice-controls-youview-apps-blind-accessibility_M12481.html

26 https://nest.com/uk/thermostat/life-with-nest-thermostat

27 https://fortune.com/2015/02/01/disabled-smart-homes

28 http://blog.laptopmag.com/smartphone-app-helps-the-blind-go-to-the-movies

29 www.slideshare.net/lmorenolopez/inclusion-of-accessibility-requirements-in-the-design-of-electronic-guides-for-museums

30 iOS accessibility guidelines are at: https://developer.apple.com/design/human-interface-guidelines/accessibility/overview/introduction
Android accessibility guidelines are at: http://developer.android.com/guide/topics/ui/accessibility/index.html
Windows Phone accessibility guidelines are at: http://msdn.microsoft.com/en-GB/library/windows/apps/hh700407.aspx
BlackBerry accessibility guidelines are at: https://developer.blackberry.com/native/documentation/best_practices/accessibility/accessibility_tools.html

31 https://in.reuters.com/article/apple-mobilephone-accessibility/advocates-for-blind-deaf-want-more-from-apple-idINKBN0FE12O20140709

32 www.slideshare.net/GeorgeZamfir/responsive-web-design-a-tool-for-accessibility

33 www.theatlantic.com/technology/archive/2014/04/what-the-shift-to-mobile-means-for-blind-news-consumers/361062

34 www.bbc.co.uk/guidelines/futuremedia/accessibility/mobile/recommendations

Activity 3

1. https://developer.apple.com/design/human-interface-guidelines /accessibility/overview/introduction
2. https://developer.android.com/guide/topics/ui/accessibility
3. www.hassellinclusion.com/blog/web-accessibility-myths -2011-part2/#text and https://www.hassellinclusion.com/blog /accessibility-myths-2019-podcast
4. www.iso.org/iso/catalogue_detail.htm?csnumber=52075
5. www.hassellinclusion.com/blog/accessibility-myths-2011/ #usability-vs-accessibility
6. http://en.wikipedia.org/wiki/Usability#Definition
7. www.forbes.com/sites/ninaangelovska/2019/01/20/gamification -trends-for-2019-making-room-for-game-elements-in-politics/ #70b84d012a77
8. www.youtube.com/watch?v=2hIjkSn477k
9. www.bbc.co.uk/guidelines/futuremedia/technical/browser _support.shtml
10. www.w3.org/TR/UAAG20
11. www.hassellinclusion.com/topics/native-element-accessibility
12. https://en.wikipedia.org/wiki/UC_Browser
13. www.bbc.co.uk/guidelines/futuremedia/technical/browser _support.shtml
14. http://modernizr.com/docs
15. www.freedomscientific.com/products/software/jaws
16. www.nvaccess.org/about-nvda
17. www.bbc.co.uk/guidelines/futuremedia/accessibility/screenreader .shtml
18. http://webaim.org/projects/screenreadersurvey
19. https://accessibility.blog.gov.uk/2016/11/01/results-of-the-2016-gov -uk-assistive-technology-survey
20. www.digitala11y.com/screen-readers-browsers-which-is-the-best -combination-for-accessibility-testing

Activity 4

1. www.w3.org/TR/UNDERSTANDING-WCAG20/understanding -techniques.html
2. https://cordova.apache.org
3. https://vimeo.com
4. www.brightcove.com
5. https://disqus.com
6. www.w3.org/WAI/intro/atag.php
7. www.hassellinclusion.com
8. www.hassellinclusion.com/blog/accessibility-2019-standards-cms -frameworks-design-thinking/#enablers
9. www.fcc.gov/events/accessing-social-media

10   www.facebook.com/accessibility
11   www.w3.org/2012/07/wcag2pas-pr.html
12   www.w3.org/TR/WCAG21
13   www-users.cs.york.ac.uk/~cpower/pubs
     /2012CHIPowerFreireGuidelines.pdf
14   http://openconcept.ca/blog/mgifford/wcag-20-aaa-journey-not
     -destination
15   https://ec.europa.eu/digital-single-market/en/web-accessibility
16   http://openconcept.ca/blog/mgifford/aoda-wcag-20-when-it
     -matters
17   www.section508.gov/manage/laws-and-policies
18   www.w3.org/TR/wai-aria
19   www.w3.org/WAI/intro/atag.php
20   http://gameaccessibilityguidelines.com
21   www.w3.org/TR/WCAG20-TECHS/flash.html
22   www.pdfa.org/publication/pdfua-in-a-nutshell
23   https://en.wikipedia.org/wiki/EPUB
24   www.hassellinclusion.com/blog/wcag-2-1-whats-in-it-for-you
25   www.bbc.co.uk/guidelines/futuremedia/accessibility/mobile
     _access.shtml
26   www.w3.org/WAI/intro/wai-age-literature
27   www.lgma.ca/assets/Programs~and~Events/Clerks~Forum/2013
     ~Clerks~Forum/COMMUNICATIONS-Making-Your-Website
     -Senior-Friendly--Tip-Sheet.pdf
28   www.w3.org/TR/UNDERSTANDING-WCAG20/conformance
     .html
29   http://openconcept.ca/blog/mgifford/wcag-20-aaa-journey-not
     -destination
30   www.w3.org/TR/UNDERSTANDING-WCAG20/intro.html
     #introduction-fourprincs-head
31   www.w3.org/TR/WCAG/#time-based-media
32   www.w3.org/TR/UNDERSTANDING-WCAG20/conformance
     .html
33   www.w3.org/TR/2008/REC-WCAG20-20081211/#conformance
     -partial
34   www.hassellinclusion.com/blog/web-accessibility-ruinous
     -obligation
35   www.hassellinclusion.com/blog/clear-eu-accessibility-law/
     #owners
36   www.hassellinclusion.com/blog/wcag-future
37   www.section508.gov/manage/laws-and-policies
38   http://mandate376.standards.eu/standard
39   www.itic.org/policy/accessibility/vpat
40   www.slideshare.net/jonathanhassell/case-studies-of-implementing
     -bs-8878-csun-2012-12145101/33

Activity 5

1   www.bbc.co.uk/accessibility
2   www.slideshare.net/jonathanhassell/2010-mydisplay-accessibility
    -preferences-arent-for-sissies
3   www.imsglobal.org/pressreleases/pr100524.html
4   www.restylethis.com
5   www.w3.org/TR/UNDERSTANDING-WCAG20/visual-audio
    -contrast-visual-presentation.html
6   www.w3.org/WAI/WCAG21/Understanding/text-spacing.html
7   www.slideshare.net/jonathanhassell/2010-mydisplay
    -accessibility-preferences-arent-for-sissies and www.slideshare.net
    /jonathanhassell/20131108-ucd13jhassellslideshare
8   www.tader.info
9   www.nintendo.com/switch/online-service/app
10 www.fcbarcelona.com/en/tickets/camp-nou-experience/plan-your
    -visit
11 www.youtube.com/watch?v=Hdtf4qUWos4
12 www.hassellinclusion.com/blog/beyond-inclusion-and-reverse
    -inclusion

Activity 6

1   https://en.wikipedia.org/wiki/Scrum_(software_development)
2   www.atlassian.com/software/jira
3   https://trello.com
4   www.incentergy.de/blog/2014/10/13/
    project-risk-management-do-risky-tasks-first
5   www.atlassian.com/software/confluence
6   http://webaim.org/resources/contrastchecker
7   http://contrast-finder.tanaguru.com
8   www.eclipse.org/actf/downloads/tools/aDesigner
9   www.bbc.co.uk/accessibility/guides/text_larger/browser
10 http://wave.webaim.org/toolbar
11 Some examples, in no particular order, and with no implied
    endorsement:
    https://developers.google.com/web/tools/lighthouse
    www.deque.com/products/worldspace
    https://tenon.io
    www.levelaccess.com/solutions/software/amp
    www.compliancesheriff.com
12 www.deque.com/axe
13 www.w3.org/WAI/eval/conformance.html
14 www.slideshare.net/jonathanhassell/2008-ux-research-design
    -and-testing-for-all-models-for-bringing-accessibility-and-usability
    -together

15 http://alistapart.com/article/quick-and-dirty-remote-user-testing
16 www.interaction-design.org/literature/article/
     how-to-conduct-a-cognitive-walkthrough
17 www.inclusivedesigntoolkit.com
18 www.hassellinclusion.com/topics/native-element-accessibility
19 www.marcozehe.de/articles/how-to-use-nvda-and-firefox-to-test
     -your-web-pages-for-accessibility
20 www.hassellinclusion.com/contact-us
21 www.deque.com/products/amaze
22 https://overlaysdontwork.com
23 http://mashable.com/2011/12/11/old-web-design
24 http://in.reuters.com/article/2014/07/09/
     apple-mobilephone-accessibility-idINKBN0FE12O20140709
25 www.hassellinclusion.com/blog/glad-cnn-closed-captions-lawsuit

Activity 7

1 www.gov.uk/government/publications/
    sample-accessibility-statement/
    sample-accessibility-statement-for-a-fictional-public-sector-website
2 www.bbc.co.uk/accessibility/index.shtml
3 www.w3.org/WAI/users/browsing
4 www.w3.org/WAI/users/inaccessible
5 www.hassellinclusion.com/blog/accessibility-accreditation-value
6 www.bbc.co.uk/blogs/bbcinternet/2009/10/
    bbc_iplayer_gets_more_audio_de.html
7 www.hassellinclusion.com/blog/write-accessibility-statement
8 www.hassellinclusion.com/accessibility-statement

Activity 8

1 https://support.google.com/youtube/answer/2734799?hl=en-GB
2 http://amara.org/en
3 www.w3.org/WAI/intro/atag.php
4 www.hassellinclusion.com/blog/relearnability-disabled-users

Acknowledgements

A book such as this is never the work of a lone writer. I am indebted to a huge number of people who have inspired me and given me the opportunity to build up the knowledge that I've aimed to share in this book.

Though I am sure I will forget someone, I'd like to especially thank the following people:

- God, for making it all happen

- My wife Rosnah for being my best friend, inspiration, confidante and touchstone

- My son Robbie for giving up being read numerous books at bedtime so that Daddy could lock himself in a room and write his own book

- My great team at Hassell Inclusion for their dedication to our common passion and their great conversations to sharpen up the ideas in this book

- Our Hassell Inclusion clients, whose engagement with accessibility and with ISO 30071-1 and BS 8878 keeps us learning every day

- Val, Norman and Moya for arranging and hosting my writing retreats so graciously

- All of my interview contributors – experts in my Hassell Inclusion team, Andrew Arch, Graham Armfield, Jennison Asuncion, David Banes, Judith Fellowes, Steve Green, Brian Kelly, Shannon Kelly, Axel Leblois, Sarah Lewthwaite, Debra Ruh, Rob Wemyss and Martin Wright – for their time and insights

- Rachel Sweetman, for checking all my references

- The Silverton Road 'Dream Journey' crowd in whose company the idea for the video blogs accompanying this book arrived

- My co-editors of 30071-1, Jim Carter and Andy Heath, and the members of ISO/IEC JTC 1, Information technology, Subcommittee SC 35, User interfaces for their insights and dedication to help take a British Standard and make it work internationally

- My IST/45 committee at BSI, who brought their considerable expertise, passion and stamina to our three-year journey to BS 8878

- Richard Titus, who shared my vision for bringing the usability and accessibility disciplines together and hired me to do just that at the BBC

- My team of usability and accessibility specialists at the BBC for joining me on my initial journey in accessibility with such good humour and skill

- Anne Eastgate and Derek Butler, who gave me the time and money to research deep into the needs of disabled children and create the solutions and techniques that are still the underpinning of all my innovation work

- Martin Wright, Richard England and the Gamelab crew for being my partners in innovation and always seeing a challenge as an opportunity

The Author

 Professor Jonathan Hassell is one of the top digital usability and accessibility thought leaders in the world. He has over eighteen years' experience in identifying new directions and challenges in digital accessibility, finding best-practice process and technology solutions to these challenges, authoring international standards and presenting best practices to conference audiences across the world.

He is the lead author of ISO 30071-1 and BS 8878.

Jonathan also leads Hassell Inclusion's team of experts providing strategic accessibility transformation services to organisations worldwide.

He specialises in training and consultancy to embed accessibility strategically within the software development lifecycle process, leadership of innovative digital projects to make inclusion easier and cheaper to implement, and creation of best-practice international web standards.

He is the former Head of Usability and Accessibility, BBC Future Media, where he combined the disciplines to embed inclusive user-centred design across web, mobile and IPTV product creation. He has won awards for product managing the accessibility features of BBC iPlayer, the accessibility personalisation tool MyDisplay, the accessibility information site My Web My Way, the uKinect Makaton sign-language games and the Nepalese Necklace mobility games for blind and partially sighted children.

He, his wife Rosnah and their son Robbie make their home in the 'garden of England', Kent.

You can find Jonathan online at:

🌐 www.hassellinclusion.com
🐦 @jonhassell
in linkedin.com/in/jonathanhassell